Four Walls against the Wind

Finding our Alaska Dream

Marge Hermans Osborn

Other books by this author:

Robert H. Armstrong and Marge Hermans
ALASKA'S NATURAL WONDERS
SOUTHEAST ALASKA'S NATURAL WORLD
LIFE AROUND MENDENHALL GLACIER
WHISTLERS ON THE MOUNTAINS
ALONG THE MOUNT ROBERTS TRAIL

Robert H. Armstrong, John Hudson, and Marge Hermans
DRAGONS IN THE POND

Robert H. Armstrong, Richard L. Carstensen,
Mary E. Willson, and Marge Hermans Osborn
THE MENDENHALL WETLANDS

Edited by Roger W. Pearson and Marge Hermans
ALASKA IN MAPS: A THEMATIC ATLAS

"Four Walls against the Wind: Finding our Alaska Dream," by Marge Hermans Osborn. ISBN 978-1-60264-442-7. Library of Congress Number on file with Publisher.

Published 2009 by Virtualbookworm.com Publishing Inc., P.O. Box 9949, College Station, TX 77842, US. ©2009, Marge Hermans Osborn. All rights reserved. No part of this publication may be reproduced, stored in a retrieval system, or transmitted in any form or by any means, electronic, mechanical, recording or otherwise, without the prior written permission of Marge Hermans Osborn.

Manufactured in the United States of America.

Contents

Preface

Where do they come from, those dreams and hoped-for's that shape our lives? What prompts us to work for years at jobs we might not even like, or to travel thousands of miles from our homes and families in search of something—something as clear as a snow-spangled peak against blue sky, or unfathomable as a landscape wrapped in the swirl of sea fog?

My dreams started in earliest childhood when for family vacations my parents and I would spend a week or a long weekend in small rental cabins or "cottages" along the Maine seacoast or in New Hampshire's White Mountains. I loved those times, when my parents had days away from demanding jobs to take walks in the woods or on the beach. We'd pick blueberries, or gather autumn leaves, then head back to our cozy little playhouse to cook dinner and spend a quiet evening reading or playing board games, just the three of us. I loved those cabins, with their worn overstuffed chairs or maple rockers, their mismatched dishes and tableware, and the soft light of old-fashioned lamps glowing on the wood of honey-colored walls.

Years later, curled up within the pink-flowered walls of my bedroom in an old Victorian house in Massachusetts, I became enthralled with books that Jack London and others wrote about life in the Far North. I loved the adventure of them, the sense of being part of a new frontier, and the descriptions of a land full of open space, strong people, and startling natural beauty.

I suppose those images were enhanced by the stories I read about pioneers in the American West. Something appealed about building a home from scratch through your own effort, tilling new ground and learning to feed yourself from it, and living in a setting where natural things, not people and machines, were your focus and your surroundings every day.

During my college years, as I studied English and American literature, I gravitated toward reading American philosophical nature writers, like Emerson, Thoreau, and Henry Beston. They wrote about finding things bigger than yourself in nature, learning to do things on your own, and living the simple life. It seemed to me that Alaska was one of the last places in the U.S. where you could still do that, and I dreamed of living there to see if that was so.

I finally made it to Alaska in 1974, but it took me twelve years to find the partner who had a dream similar to my own, and another eight years for us to find a place where we might be able to make our shared dreams come true.

Now I'm grateful for every day I live amid the spectacular and awe-inspiring landscape of Southeast Alaska. And I'm grateful to live in a country that gives me the freedom and the economic opportunity to build this life that satisfies my deepest longings and most heartfelt desires. I'm grateful for the fervent dreams of a few New England settlers, and for succeeding generations of Americans who clung to those dreams and nurtured them through prosperity and despair.

I think there are few human beings so abused and downtrodden that they have no dreams, and all our dreams are wonderfully different. I would not want everyone to share my dream, even if that were possible. But I do hope that by writing about our experience I can inspire those bold in spirit (or not so bold!) to strike out in search of their own dreams, in the same way that books I read and people I met during my growing years inspired me to do the same.

Thank you to the many, many people who have helped me along the way, to the teachers and writing companions who encouraged me and helped me improve my writing, and especially to Tom, who has helped me come, beyond mere geography, to where I've always longed to be.

Southeast Alaska

Southeast Alaska, the Panhandle of the 49th State, includes some 2,000 islands. Ranging in size from Prince of Wales, which is slightly larger than the state of Delaware, to rocky outcrops barely rising above sea level, they make up nearly half the land area of the region.

1.
From the Ground Up

August 7, 1994
to
June 5, 1995

Devil's club

1994, August to December

August 7 – We've found it—a beautiful place in a remote setting where we can finally begin building our dream cabin. We've bought a little less than an acre of land in a bay of one of the big islands between Juneau and the outer coast. We overlook a tiny, crescent-shaped cove between two marble reefs that reach out into the bay like knobby arms. From the beach we look across a mile of water to two little islands and a heavily forested shoreline, and beyond that to the Chilkat Mountains— jagged peaks that rise above Lynn Canal like the backdrop for a Sigmund Romberg musical.

This is one of several plots of private land clustered in this small bay—remnants of cannery property, mining claims, and homesteads that were individually owned before most of Southeast Alaska was designated Tongass National Forest. We feel lucky to have found it, and grateful that the owners were willing to sell to us. Tom chose this lot from among several others because it has a little stream and a broad, gentle slope up from the beach.

It was wonderful to spend the weekend just trying to get acquainted with the land—our future homesite, we hope! Apparently the area was partially logged many years ago, but now it has a wonderful variety of vegetation. There are patches of bright green where ferns and small understory plants grow. Above them, scattered red alder trees stretch skyward, often at weird angles. Patches of blueberries and other tall shrubs crowd beneath mixed alders, spruce, and hemlock. And there's one long stretch of towering spruce and hemlocks where the light is dim beneath the tall canopy, and your footsteps are muffled by a carpet of fallen needles.

The little stream is less than a foot wide, but it flows out of the woods from the back to the front of the lot in lovely, winding curves, slipping around and under fallen logs and roots, and emerging in bubbly riffles, stretches of smooth water, and two deep pools filled by tiny waterfalls. Just above the beach are five or six big old drift logs covered with moss and small spruce and hemlock seedlings. At the south end, the beach broadens into a grassy meadow that surrounds a tiny pond.

The trip from town in *Dauntless* took about 2-1/2 hours, all 30 feet of the boat slipping gracefully through the water. What a luxury to sit in the warm cabin drinking coffee, or to step out on the back deck to watch the panorama go by. It's a classic inside water trip in Southeast Alaska. We glide past forested shoreline with eagles perched in spruce trees, turn past the red-roofed lighthouse at Pt. Retreat, then cruise along the blue-water ribbon of Lynn Canal, and around three rocky islands guarding the mouth of the bay. There's a state float about a quarter mile from the lot, so we can tie up there, then shuttle to our beachfront in our inflatable dinghy.

The inflatable is too heavy to haul up and down the beach, so one of our first chores was to set up an outhaul, the device folks here use to tether their skiffs and small boats to keep them afloat at every stage of the tide. It's a challenge, since the tides here range more than 20 feet between high and low in the course of the year. This weekend's tides are far from the lowest of the year, but at low tide the water dropped nearly 300 yards from the top of the beach, leaving a long stretch of rocks and mud at its lowest ebb.

Our outhaul runs in a triangle between three anchor points: a large Danforth anchor buried beneath a pile of rocks at low tide level, and two posts planted parallel to shore at the top of the beach. The posts are made from a tall flagpole-size hemlock Tom cut on the lot. They're about 15 feet apart and planted several feet deep into the beach just above high tide line. Each of the three anchor points has a pulley attached, and passing through them all is about 700 feet of 3/8-inch braided, lead-cored polyester line that Tom spliced into a continuous loop.

We fastened a tether of nylon line to the bow of the inflatable, and Tom spliced on two stainless steel clips like the ones halibut fishermen use on their longline gear. When we fasten the clips onto the outhaul loop, the inflatable can be pulled out into deep water while we're ashore, then pulled in to the beach when we're ready to leave.

Up on land we've cleared our first path up from shore, following the north bank of the stream. It's hard to believe how many dead branches, logs, and stumps are scattered over the ground. You have to marvel at the sheer quantity of material these trees have produced and discarded over only a few decades. In some places the brush is also thick, and it's difficult to wade through it to see what the terrain is like.

But Tom thinks he's decided on a cabin site. It's on a bench about 60 feet back from the top of the beach that he thinks is well drained and fairly level. I'd hoped to be closer to the beach for the view, but it will be nice to be back among the trees where the cabin might not be noticed from the water. The little stream runs just to the north of the bench, so we should be able to hear it through open windows.

We also hauled in a packing crate that Tom has turned upright on the short end to make a place to put our tools—Swede saws, shovels, pickax, and whatever else we find we need. Tom mounted it on four notched alder logs so it will be movable, covered it with black roofing paper, and put on a piece of delta-rib roofing to keep off the rain. It looks like a tarpaper shack from an Appalachian "holler," but I suppose it's a fitting beginning for our modest plans.

Saw a varied thrush in the woods and some Canada geese on the beach meadow. Heard a ruby-crowned kinglet in the trees next to the stream, and a blue grouse hooting back east toward the mountain.

August 15 – Tom's dad, his sister Lucy, and her husband John are visiting, and they're all enthusiastic about our choice of property. Pops has claimed the rocky outcrop on the north end of the beach as his "settin' place." Every once in a while he'll turn up missing, and when we look for him he's out there gazing out over the water and smoking his pipe. Tom said his dad always reminisced about his time in Seward during World War II, and that he'd always wanted to come back to Alaska. I guess in a small way this is his chance.

Everyone's helping us with clearing. We hauled three big piles of brush and deadwood to the beach, and had a great bonfire. Then we tackled a big spruce stump sitting right in the middle of the cabin site. I swear that stub from some big old tree was the size of a small Volkswagen. At waist height, where the trunk had been cut, it was more than three feet across the top, and it had four big lateral roots that arched down and spread out lengthways like gigantic talons clutching the ground.

We figure the tree must have been cut at least sixty or seventy years ago. Maybe it made pilings or supports for the cannery or the mine that operated in the bay during its heyday; or maybe it helped form one of the big fish traps that were set out at the mouth of the bay to catch salmon to supply the cannery. At any rate, the original tree must have been at least 100 feet tall and two or three hundred years old. Even in this wet climate, the stump had rotted only about an inch deep around the outer surface. Beneath that, it was as solid as an oak table. We could only imagine the load it had supported as 100 feet of massive trunk and hundreds of outspread branches stretched above the forest floor through rain, heavy snow, and winds of 50 knots and more in the winter. Now this massive chunk of the base is all that's left.

We decided the best way to begin was to cut off the lateral roots, then chip away at the main stump. John, Lucy, and I started out with shovels, a rake, a pickax, and a long-handled garden scratcher, pulling back as much dirt as we could from around the base. As we exposed the roots, Tom cut off whatever parts of them he could reach with the chain saw. Once we'd tunneled under and around a root we'd wrap it with the chain of the come-along (a contraption of chains and gears that can pull up to 4,000 pounds), then Tom or John cranked on the come-along handle to try to break the root free.

It was hard, heavy work. Sometimes as the pressure on the chain built up we'd hear a snap and the stump would move what seemed a fraction of an inch, or we'd hear a louder snap and with a terrible shudder the stump would move an inch or more. When things stopped moving, and Tom or John couldn't crank any more, they'd release the chain and we'd go after another of the big lateral roots with the chain saw, dig out some more around the base, then hook up the chain and try cranking again.

Tom is used to working around heavy equipment. He knows the capacities and limitations of his tools, and he's extremely conscious of safety. But I found working with such massive weights and pressures frightening. It was nerve-wracking to stand off to the side while Tom hefted and cranked, yet the huge stump stood immobile and I imagined pound after pound of pressure building against the chain. The chain pulled so tight I thought it would surely snap, slashing out at one of us, or slapping back against a nearby tree. You could hear the chain slowly ratcheting around the spool, *scrr...ack, scrr...ack, scrr ...ack,* and the sudden hollow rips and snaps as the big stump groaned and tore free bit by bit from the ground. All this took place against the burbling of the stream and the squawking of ravens and crows in the big spruce grove on the point to the south of us.

Except for one afternoon that Lucy and I took off to go fishing, it took the four us nearly two and a half days to get that stump out. It's pulled off to the side of the cabin site now, a giant bruised knuckle the size of a washing machine, its roots cut off and dragged away to the burn pile.

August 28 – We've dug out a dozen or more stumps and cut down brush and some thirty alders to clear a 20-by-30-foot cabin site. Most of the alders are six to eight inches in diameter and will make a nice beginning to our firewood supply. We have five stacks of bucked-up stove wood piled between pairs of trees to dry over the winter.

November 10 – Back in town now, and shut out of work on the cabin for the winter, but Tom has begun drawing up plans. He says he learned drafting skills in high school, and I guess he's been building things and working with tools since he was a kid. It helps that he knows standard sizes of lumber, and how to construct things so you waste as little material as possible. He thinks 16-by-24 feet would be a good cabin size, and he's building a cardboard model to give us a feel of how the space could be divided into kitchen, bathroom, and living areas. We'll need a wood stove right away, so he's bought a kit to make one from a 55-gallon drum. It will have a square metal door in one end and a stovepipe at the top.

December 27 – Tom bought me this beautiful hard-cover Thomas Kincaid journal for Christmas. He said he thought I could keep my notes about building the cabin in it. The cover shows a log cabin with a dreamy quality and ethereal light. Soft, golden light streams from the windows, and the cabin is set beneath overhanging evergreens, with a canoe pulled up on a beach. I know it's a terribly romanticized image of what Tom and I have dreamed about for so long, but it captures the feel of what I've longed for all these years. It's exciting to think we have a chance to make it happen.

1995, Early January to June 5

January 10 – Still in town and enjoying our research into potential cabin plans and pre-packaged cedar cabins. We talked by phone today with folks at Pan Abode, a company south of Seattle that has built a number of rustic cabins for the Forest Service in Alaska. They're willing to adapt one of their basic cabin plans to include the extra windows and roof overhangs we feel we need to have for this climate. Tom likes their "Phoenix System"— outer and inner walls of tongue-and-groove cedar with solid foam insulation between. It has the look and feel of a log cabin without the impracticalities, and Tom thinks the main roof beam is small enough that the two of us can get it up by ourselves. The plans will be engineered to account for snow load and wind shear, and, best of all, everything we need—wall timbers, interior siding, metal roofing, doors and windows, hardware and glue—can be shipped from Seattle in a single package. We won't be on our own, 60 miles round trip by boat from the nearest hardware store, trying to figure out what we need next. We've scheduled delivery for mid-June—from Seattle to Juneau by barge, then from Juneau to the cabin site by landing craft. Meanwhile, we'll be responsible for putting in the foundation up to floor level.

January 12 – Picked up our first load of discarded power poles from the yard of the local electrical utility. Tom thinks they'll make perfect pilings for the cabin foundation. They're sturdy—between 12 and 16 inches in diameter—and he says they'll eliminate the need to haul in and mix innumerable sacks of concrete for a cement foundation. We chose the best ones of yellow cedar, which Tom says is very strong and resists rot. We pulled out sixteen of the best-looking ones from the discard pile and cut them into 8-foot lengths. The Chevy pickup can carry eight at a time before the tires start flattening.

March 26 – Final plans arrived from Pan Abode today— front, back, and side views of the cabin with a fat sheaf of building instructions and long, detailed lists of the materials we'll receive for everything from the floor up. Tom is poring over them and trying to help me make some sense of the different views and specifications.

March 28 – Drove home from a meeting downtown today, and my heart tingled when I saw the thirty-five cedar poles heaped in our front yard under a frosting of snow. What a sense of excitement and satisfaction! Tom says we'll float them over to the cabin site first thing in the spring.

April 14 – Got *Dauntless* out of winter storage and into the water. I'm proud of our winter's work: She looks spiffy and eager to run with a new coat of bottom paint, polish on the hull and superstructure, and a refurbished engine. Tom is working 10-day shifts, commuting by floatplane to the hydroplant 40 miles south of town. That means we'll have to do our cabin work on four-day weekends and vacation days, including commuting time from town to the site. I hope we get good weather for boating and building.

April 20 – Took all the foundation poles down to the harbor today. Our friends Bruce and Fran, who have their own remote cabin on Shelter Island, helped us haul them to Auke Bay harbor with their big pickup. We backed each truckload down the boat ramp and skidded the logs into the water. Then Tom maneuvered around them in the inflatable dinghy, stringing them together with six-inch spikes and lengths of galvanized chain to form a raft five logs wide and seven logs long. We got permission from the harbormaster to anchor them on the outside of the breakwater so long as they're flagged and we're sure to move them by early tomorrow morning. I think I will pray all night that the four-foot seas forecast for tomorrow don't build up till afternoon.

April 21 – Enroute to the cabin site at last. We got an early start at 6 a.m. So far we've had flat calm, and the forecast has changed to winds less than 15 knots. We've been underway for four hours now, making a slow 4 to 5 knots while the raft follows like an oversized duckling waddling behind its mother. The fluorescent orange flags Tom put on it to mark the corners dip and flutter against a backdrop of gentle waves and distant snow-covered mountains. So we don't have to live my nightmare of coasting the shoreline of Lynn Canal in the dinghy to corral thirty-five bobbing hunks of cedar broken loose from their tethers. I'm surprised the raft bobbles along so nicely, considering it weighs half as much as the boat and is half again as long.

2 p.m. - Rounding the point and entering the bay.

7 p.m. - The foundation poles are beached. We'd hoped for a high tide so we could float them to the top of the beach in front of the cabin, but this week's tides are only medium high—12-footers rather than the ideal 18- or 20-. Oh well, every inch helps. High tide was at 5:55 p.m. Tom unhitched the raft from the big boat and maneuvered it with the inflatable, pulling it as far up the beach as it would go, then he anchored it to two stakes he pounded into the beach. The poles are lying catawampus among the rocks and seaweed, gray and glistening as beached seals. Tom says each one weighs about 150 pounds. How on earth are we going to get them all up the beach?

Spent the afternoon clearing more brush and ferrying ashore parts for our next project: assembling a 4-by-8-foot workshop and toolshed that Tom measured and cut back in town. We've established a route for hauling the foundation posts up to the staging area near the cabin site. Remnants of an old logging road make a natural path up the slope, and there's a clear area beneath several big spruce trees where we can stack the posts out of the way for now.

April 22 – We started dragging the foundation logs off the beach this morning. First we pried them loose from the spikes and chains and stacked them on the beach. Then Tom carried the logs one by one across the beach mud to solid ground above high tide level. It's painful to watch him hefting those big things, but he seems to think it's OK. Once he gets a log up into the grass, we lay it across a pair of 8-inch rubber wheels Tom welded to a free-swinging metal axle with a pull rope attached at each side. We maneuver the log to its balance point, then strap it to the axle with a 2-inch rayon strap and ratcheting buckle. Then Tom pulls the whole contraption up the slope to the stockpile.

We kept experimenting to find the easiest way. Sometimes the two of us would yoke up to the wheels, a couple of oxen huffing and pulling in tandem. I distracted myself by counting the 150 steps it took to drag each load to the stockpile. We laugh a lot and have christened the wheels and axle "The Wheels o'Death."

April 23 – Moving foundation poles again today. We've finished three rows, but as we move each one, the remaining rows sit about 10 feet lower down the beach and have to be moved farther. This morning, as his energy for lifting flagged, Tom tried tipping the logs end over end instead of carrying them, but they splattered mud all over us every time they crashed onto the beach, and Tom soon ran out of energy for lifting and heaving. Finally he suggested we build a "Michigan Logger's Road."

We'd saved 6-foot lengths of some of the small alders we cut in clearing the cabin site last summer, so this was a good chance to use them. We hauled ten of them down to the beach and laid them crosswise in front of the remaining raft of fifteen logs. Tom wrapped the come-along around a big rock high on the beach and hooked the other end to the lead chain on the raft. As he cranked on the lever of the come-along, the entire log raft skidded and jerked, inch by inch, up the alder pole road. Meanwhile, I stumbled through the sticky mud, rushing to keep up with the raft's steady progress so I could pull up poles freed up at the back end of the raft and lay them down in front.

April 24 – Moved the last of the foundation poles today. They make an impressive pile in the staging area. Tom's marked the exact location of the cabin and squared off the measurements with posts and string. We've dug the holes for fourteen foundation poles and set posts into ten of them. Each post has to be seated solid to provide good support, so the holes have to be 3 to 3-1/2 feet deep. Tom and I have developed different methods of digging, partly because of our different body strength and partly because we have only one of most tools. He digs faster than I do, using our only posthole digger. Once he's started the first few inches of a hole with a miner's pick and a shovel, he slams the digger to the bottom of the hole, grabs chunks of earth between the two clamshells, lifts them, and drops them next to the top of the hole. Each time he does it I can see his back muscles flexing with the effort. *Thunk!* Lift. Drop. *Thunk!* Lift. Drop. I'm amazed he can keep doing it, time and time again.

I take a different approach that's easier on my back. If I kneel down and work with small garden tools, I can excavate holes at least 2 feet deep so Tom has to dig only the bottom foot or so. I use the miner's pick, a metal scratcher, a trowel, and—because it's the best thing I could find to scoop soil with—a plastic bucket left over from our last one-pint purchase of raspberry jam.

I can tell you I now know in my bones every layer of the ground our cabin will sit on. The top layer is brown-ish-black soil that smells rich and looks like a farmer's dream. I imagine it as duff, humus, rot of alder leaves, and the remains of whatever evergreen needles, insects, squirrels, deer, and bears have died here over the years. I think of it as holding dead berries, fallen lichens, and the rain, snow, and sunlight of hundreds of seasons. Almost invariably damp, it grinds into our clothing and work gloves like black grease.

There's an incredible network of roots tangled and woven together in this layer. No matter where we dig, we run into clusters of alder roots. They're often wrapped together with the red-skinned roots of nearby spruce trees and saplings, and I keep running into buried chunks of broken roots and branches that must be scrap left behind from logging. Digging through this stuff is like trying to cut through a combination of nylon fishing net, chicken wire, and an occasional twisted up two-by-four. Thank goodness for pruning shears, long-handled loppers, and (for big roots) a hand saw. My work progresses only inches at a time.

That soil layer is usually between four and six inches deep. Beneath it is either coarse, gravelly sand with fist-sized rocks in it, or a mixture of small rocks crammed together like the aggregate of pebbles and concrete you sometimes see in urban buildings or walkways. There are only a few roots there, so I can put away my pruning shears and cutting tools. But the gravel and rocks are packed tight, and after the first few inches the blade of the pick won't fit within the 10-inch confines of the hole anymore. I finally ended up using the little garden scratcher to loosen the gravel, but it makes a horrible *scritching* sound like fingernails on a blackboard. What a relief when I can finally scoop out a bucketful.

Tom thinks this bench is the old beach line, maybe just above high tide when the land was lower or sea level was higher. I imagine it being smashed and ground under tons of glacier ice centuries ago, with rocks and gravel dragged from the mountain out back down the slope toward the sea.

May 3 – Tom's been spending many of his hours off shift at the hydroplant gathering building materials and loading them onto *Dauntless*, which we're using on some weekends to commute between the plant site and the harbor at Auke Bay. Last week we loaded up a stack of 2-by-4s and twenty 2-by-8s Tom had cut from a downed spruce using his chain saw sawmill last fall. We hauled them to Auke Bay, then picked up additional gear to go to the cabin site. This morning poor *Dauntless* looks like a freight barge, with stacks of lumber, two 55-gallon blue plastic water barrels, the gas generator we bought to run power tools, two 5-gallon plastic fuel jugs, and boxes of supplies for the weekend.

May 4 – 10:20 p.m. Tied up at the state float, feeling the wind and watching the stars. It was a long evening trip from town, and we arrived after dark. The boat is tossing and turning—westerly swells are rolling in from somewhere off the outer coast. A quarter moon is glinting on the water, and there are pinpricks of stars, but the wind is whistling at the windows and water is slapping against the hull. I have to step back from chores—lighting the stove, mixing up sourdough for tomorrow morning's pancakes, making up our bed in the V-berth—to remember why we are here. I feel exposed here on the water, and I long to be on shore in a snug cabin, sitting out the wind in the shelter of the trees.

May 5 – Got up at 4:45 a.m. to ferry the 12-foot-long 2-by-8s ashore at the height of the tide. We hauled ten planks in each of two loads, dragging them in the spare fiberglass skiff behind the inflatable with its 4-horse-power outboard. The first trip was frustrating. The fiberglass skiff wouldn't drag behind us in a straight line. It seesawed in long, undulating S-curves, probably tripling the time and energy it took to travel the quarter mile to the beach. By the time we made the second trip, we'd figured out we could hold the loaded skiff tight to the side of the inflatable, and it traveled much better.

On both trips we met curious seals, their heads popping out of the water behind or to the side of us like small bowling balls with big brown eyes. Saw a loon, still in gray and white plumage, and two shore birds. Carrying the boards up to the lot, we were greeted by bright yellow flags of newly sprouting skunk cabbage all along the marsh at the foot of the stream. What a bright, festive surprise! It reminded me to look up from working and remember that the purpose of all this effort is to settle us into surroundings like these.

May 8 – Wrapping up our second four-day weekend at the cabin site. Tom got in two strings of floor beams and half of the third row before he ran out of materials. It takes three overlapping 12-foot beams to span the length of the cabin. They're all nailed together and placed edgewise on top of a row of foundation posts. Once the beams were in place, Tom slabbed two sides of the support posts off flat, bolted a wooden plate onto each side of the beam, then bolted the beam and the plate to the post. It looks sturdy all right. I'm surprised at how meticulous Tom is about getting the beams level, trimming or shaving them if necessary. I think they must all be level within a sixteenth of an inch. Tom jokes that the deer may be concerned about the quality of our work, too. We found fresh tracks around the posts and beams every morning.

I dug three more holes where the cabin roof will overhang the back deck, and Tom fitted cedar support posts into them. We also dug a hole and backfilled a 55-gallon plastic barrel into it for the outhouse. With a hole in the top and a toilet seat fitted on, it will be sheer luxury after the previous "field camp" accommodations. We've decided the outhouse building will be 4 by 5 feet. I dug through three entwined stumps for the first foundation post and will finish the others and the two remaining cabin roof supports after the posts and string marking the cabin perimeter are down and out of the way. We also cut through several knee-high fallen logs obstructing the path at the south end of the property. We now have two trails to the beach. Kept the fire going on the burn pile long enough to get rid of all the brush we had stacked there. The next high tide should wash away the ashes.

I cleared a shallow channel for the stream to flow where the water pools up just behind the cabin site and found a beautiful little glade I had not noticed before. The stream flows around and under some big tree roots and rocks, and there are thick green hummocks of moss and little plants all along the banks. Some of the skunk cabbage there had deer nibbles on the leaves, and there were fresh deer droppings, too. With all the thickets and little plants I'll bet it's a real deer haven. What a back yard!

Tom put together the 4-by-8-foot workshop he'd laid out and cut in town. It will house our growing collection of tools and a 3.5 kilowatt gas generator to run power tools. Right now the roof's of heavy plastic sheeting (which I'm learning to properly call visqueen), but we'll replace that with clear plastic ribbed roofing when we can.

We enjoyed lots of wildlife sightings this weekend. On two different days we heard a humpback whale blowing in the bay and stopped work to run down to the beach and see it. Saw a heron on the beach twice at low tide, and a raucous gang of crows chasing a raven. We also watched a fierce fight among robins feeding on the forest floor. What a squall! There was a great shrieking and swooping of four or five birds, then one perched on a nearby branch and sang and sang and sang. Was it celebrating victory, or calling out to appeal to a female? Maybe both! The woodpecker came several times. We watched it swoop from one tree to another, hopping up or down the trunk, pecking-pecking-pecking, then moving on to test another tree. It worked on both alders and spruce and even landed on the new tool shed and pecked at the plywood. What a magnificent deep red head and chest it has, and black wings with vertical white stripes. I looked it up in Bob Armstrong's *Guide to the Birds of Alaska* and believe it's a red-breasted sapsucker.

As we were leaving the float to head back to town, Tom spotted two otters mating. They came from the water onto the beach with one following the other very closely, then they went back into the water and one climbed on the other's back. When they came out again, they seemed to be stuck together, as I've seen happen with dogs, and when they lay down together I could see something bright red, which I could only imagine was an engorged male organ. They lay together for about ten minutes, the smaller one acting as if it was uncomfortable but unable to get away. Finally they separated and moved slowly up the beach, though the larger, darker one, which I guessed might be the male, followed the smaller one very closely and seemed to be put off only because the other one appeared very resistant. I have to say the whole thing did not look like fun for either party involved!

May 10 – In town this week we talked with the owner of the landing craft that will deliver the cabin package. He said we need to clear rocks from a swath of beach 30 feet wide so he can come to shore without damaging his boat. "Nothing larger than a grapefruit" can be sticking up, he said. Oh boy. Right now the beach looks like the ragtag rubble left by a retreating glacier. There are rocks the size of breadboxes and watermelons, and a few the size of large beanbag chairs. How on earth will we clear it?

May 19 – Made it out to the cabin site with another load of stuff—sheets of plywood, 2-by-4s, panels of clear plastic roofing, groceries, tools for moving rocks, two more 55-gallon plastic barrels, and crab-pot floats for marking the channel up the beach for the landing craft. The water was calm, so we anchored in 30 feet of water in front of the lot to save time running back and forth to the float with loads of material. We found two piles of bear scat near our clearing. One looked pretty fresh. Tom found more piles down on the beach, and we could see patches of beach grass that had been chewed off at the tips. We also found several small clumps of bear hair on the end of one of the cabin beams. It looks as if deer aren't the only ones who have taken an interest in our work.

May 20 – What a chore just to build an outhouse! We carted in seven sheets of plywood, forty 2-by-4s, and two treated 2-by-6s. I'm flabbergasted that just the materials cost $345. We had to dig two trenches 5 feet long and about 6 inches deep, then bury two cedar logs to fasten the house to. Tom made a frame of 2-by-6s and a floor, then the foundation logs had to be leveled from side to side and front to back. I thought we'd never get them right. We had to move dirt, roots, and a large stump. Quit at 9:15 p.m. and went back to the boat. Had supper watching the last alpenglow light the snow-capped Chilkats and hearing a humpback whale spouting outside the window.

May 21 – Tied up at the state float. We had to move over here in the middle of the night when the wind came up. This morning as we were having breakfast we watched two bears in the grassy cove just southeast of the float. One was very large. At first I wondered if the two were a sow and adolescent cub, but at one point the smaller bear chased the larger one away. Now I wonder if the smaller one is a sow and the larger one a suitor. The smaller one was on the beach when we took the inflatable around the point to the cabin site. It barely glanced up when a float plane flew low over it for a good look. Our neighbors at the head of the bay have told us several bear stories, but the most important thing seems to be keeping your distance when you see them and never leaving any garbage or food around to attract them. The browns, which are all that we have on the island, seem to shun people more than the blacks back in town. They're unpredictable, though, and it would be easy to run into one unexpectedly, so we carry the shotgun or bear spray when we go off alone or up to the cabin site after working down on the beach. I hope we can get along with the bears as well as the old-timers here seem to. Not many people in this world get to share an island with awe-inspiring animals like these.

Today we put in the third floor beam and the last three foundation posts, with time out for bouts of moving rocks on the beach. Instead of log-rolling contests we now have rock-rolling contests. Both Tom and I are refining our techniques, and I'm determined someday to write an essay on "Fifteen Ways to Move a Rock." Depending on how big they are, we can throw them away from the swath we're trying to clear. Or we can hoist them into the wheelbarrow, bob across the lumpy beach, and dump them into piles along each side. Some we can pry loose with a long-handled crowbar, then carry or roll them outside to the edges, too.

Nearly all the rocks are buried pretty deep in the beach mud, and they make a big sucking sound once we finally pop them loose. We've discovered that a number of rocks are round but have one flat side. We dig holes beside those, then tip them into the holes so the flat side is up and the rock doesn't poke up above the beach anymore. Tom's been able to break a few of the big ones with a sledge hammer so they split into smaller pieces we can carry away. And the ones too big to move any of the usual ways we pull with the come-along.

We've found we can deal with some of the really big ones by working together. We dig around till Tom can get the shovel under one corner and break the suction, then he lifts the rock while I throw piles of small rocks underneath. The rock tips higher and higher, until we can put the come-along chain around it and drag it off to the side. The anchor rock for the come-along doesn't even have to be bigger than the one we're moving. So long as it's anchored in the mud, it will usually hold firm.

June 2 – Motored out from town this evening with our usual load of stuff. We arrived too late to do anything tonight, but briefly met the new neighbor who's building a cabin around the point from us. Hope to get an early start tomorrow. Wind and rain forecast for the weekend.

June 3 – Tom has put the transparent ribbed roofing on the toolshed. We finished clearing the beach, put up guide poles along the cleared swath, and tied surveyor's tape on the poles to mark 4 feet, 5 feet, and 6 feet above ground level. We tied on a crab-pot float to mark the one gigantic flat-topped rock we can't budge. At high tide it should have 4 feet clearance—enough for the landing craft to slip over, we think. We also cut away two drift logs, an alder, and a big stump to broaden the pathway up from the beach to the staging area. Tom finished the trim and roof edges on the outhouse and put in diagonal bracing on some of the cabin foundation beams.

I spent the day clearing behind the cabin. I cut brush and hauled out dead alder poles in the glade beside the stream, where the blueberries are trying to flourish. Worked my way across the back of the cabin site, and by the end of the day I was nibbling into the logging slash at the southeast corner. It's a matchstick jumble of downed logs with devil's club growing 12 feet high and dead menziesia brush sticking up in patches well over my head.

June 4 – A day of wild, changing weather. First it was low overcast, then squalls rode through and it poured rain. We had decided we'd better do a little more clearing on the beach, so we both got soaked by the shower. Then the sun came out—blue sky with feathery wisps of cloud. Now at 10 p.m. the sun is just going down, and there is a sliver of moon. Tom finished roofing the outhouse and the workshop, strengthened the workshop door, and set up a visqueen shelter to keep off the rain and hold a little heat from the barrel stove, which is—ah!—set up at last. After the beach project I spent the rest of the day clearing again. I think I'm getting pretty good at running the little chain saw. Got through the big snarl of slash and deadfall and rooted out the big patch of devil's club. It's good to see sunlight getting through to the ground, and I hope it will encourage blueberries and little plants the deer will like.

June 5 – Saw a large, very dark brown bear grazing in the cove as we motored back to the float this afternoon. It finally looked up and watched us, then walked away, up over a drift log and into the woods. What a thrill to be sharing our space with bears! They are such magnificent animals and seem so wild and free. I think they move out when there are lots of boats in the bay, like on weekends, then take the place back over when the two-legged critters leave. We're being extremely careful with food—storing it in the shed when we're down on the beach, leaving only granola bars and dried soup in glass jars in the shed, and taking out our garbage every night. I hope it will pay off and that we and the bears can get along well here.

Today Tom built a small bridge over the stream, connecting the materials staging area with the cabin site. He says we should run an ad for a troll to take up residence. I cut out more stumps and widened the paths around the site, then laid alder poles to set the stacks of materials up out of the mud. We're ready for the cabin delivery, and we spent our last couple of hours watching birds and walking around. It's hard to believe we'll be back in a week unloading everything, with a full seven days to get a good start on building.

2.

Building

1995 – mid-June to October

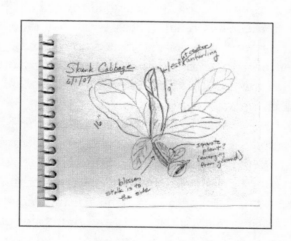

June 14 – The cabin package arrived today. Luck
was with us. This morning the water was flat calm,
with nary a flutter in the flags we'd put on the
poles marking the channel. Waiting was the hardest
part, I think—and worrying that we'd forgotten
something important in our preparations. Our
elderly neighbors Bill and Helen came by from their cabin
on the point to pick up the log splitter they'd arranged to
have shipped out along with our package. Landing craft
deliveries are expensive and hard to schedule, so it really
helps to double up when anyone's arranged a trip from
town.

A little before high tide the landing craft rounded
the far point, and we watched with our hearts pounding
as it steamed into the bay then angled toward our beach.
What a tremendous relief it was when it glided neatly
between the marker poles and nosed up to the beach. A
crew member yanked on some cables, and with a metallic
groan the bow dropped down to make a ramp and open
the deck completely for unloading.

As the skipper climbed down to start the forklift,
we got a full view of the cabin package—seven pallets
the size of small pickup trucks wrapped in black plastic.
It looked like enough materials to build two cabins. The
skipper hooked a sling around the forwardmost pallet
(marked "Osborn - 3,100 lb." in gray spray paint), pulled
it up with the forklift, and began trundling down the
ramp. The load tipped and swayed as the lift's rubber
tires rolled over bumps in the ramp. As the tires rolled
down onto the beach, the load began swaying, and with
a sickening lurch it tipped way too far out to the side. We
heard the skipper yell, "Blue clay! I should have known!"
One big rubber wheel sank deep into the mud. The load

veered sharply to the right, jerked down, and slid into the water.

Tom and I waded out, water over our boot tops, and grabbed at the huge plastic-wrapped package. "We'll have to cut it loose!" the skipper yelled, and Tom nodded. "Okay," he said, grabbing a knife out of his pocket. The skipper released the sling, and Tom cut away the strapping and plastic covering. Within seconds the water around us was littered with bobbing building materials—lengths of cedar decking, 2-by-4s, 2-by-6s, rolls of roofing paper, and three beautiful laminated beams wrapped in waxed paper. Tom and I grabbed the beams as quickly as we could and hauled them up the beach. Then we went back and gathered up armloads of whatever else we could carry. I was dismayed to see Bill, who's in his late seventies, wading out to his boot tops, too, hauling handfuls of lumber out of the water and passing them to Helen, who stacked them in a growing pile above the mud.

As Tom and I struggled to corral the runaway pieces, the skipper wrestled with the forklift and manhandled it back onto the landing craft. The tide had come in another foot or so, and the crew eased the boat higher onto the beach where there was less blue clay. The skipper slung another pallet (lighter than the first, Tom said, because the first pallet had had all the big beams) and rolled with it onto the beach and up the road to the staging area. We had to grab the chain saw and cut down one more alder, but our road ultimately proved to be wide enough, and the platforms we'd made of alder poles were perfect for keeping the pallets off the damp ground. By the time the forklift had made its third and fourth trips across the beach, though, the ground had turned into a muddy swamp. Those big tires struggled and churned in a morass of black mud, and as the loads lurched from side to side I wondered if the doors and windows would make it through this whole process without breaking apart.

Somehow Tom and the skipper got the last three loads onto the beach and up the road, while on board the landing craft the crew eased slowly backward because now the tide had turned and was going out. We unloaded Bill and Helen's log splitter, and they hauled it off with the four-wheeler and trailer they use to move heavy loads. The landing craft steamed back out the channel, while Tom and I sighed with relief that the whole process was over. Of course, it wasn't over at all. We worked till 10 p.m. stacking materials from the broken pallet and ripping the waxed paper off the big beams so they could dry out where salt water had leaked through the wrapping. I'd hoped to take video of the landing process, but everything went haywire once that first load went into the water, so I guess this account will be the best record we'll have of what happened.

June 15 – On site at 7 a.m. Still working on the cabin underpinnings. It took all day to put in four rim joists around the foundation. Tom was determined they would be absolutely level. He had to notch the beams to mate them, then notch the four corners for metal straps to attach them to the posts. I tried to inventory some of what's in the pallets, but the amount of material and the lists of lumber, fasteners, glue, roofing, and a million other components are overwhelming. We can't find the caulking gun we'll need to put in the underlayment for the floor tomorrow, but we were able to borrow one from our neighbor Phil at the head of the bay. We felt sheepish asking to borrow from someone we hardly know, but apparently he's rescued a lot of greenhorns during the twenty-five years he's lived here. He laughed when we apologized. "It's no biggie," he said. "It's the kind of thing that happens out here. You'll see."

Phil's wife Donna says everyone in the bay monitors channel 15 on the CB. They all have handles from some colorful part of their lives, like Shakemaker, Crab Pot, Whale Bone, and Bear Heaven. Phil said after the fiasco yesterday our handle should be Mudhole, but I don't want to be reminded of this experience for the next twenty years, so we'll have to think of something else. Quit at 9 p.m.

June 16 – Tough day. Pouring rain. It's a pain to work with wet lumber. Cut and put in forty-two floor joists. Each one takes toenails on two sides, with blocking on every third beam and blocking between each two joists. Too tired to write.

June 17 – Laid plywood subflooring today. What a hassle hefting those big sheets of plywood to make the tongue-and-groove edges fit. At least it's stopped raining. I unpacked and inventoried all the exterior wall timbers, which meant locating them in the pallets, pulling them out, and carrying them across the stream to the building site. Each vertical support column is numbered, and each horizontal timber is marked with a letter for the wall it fits on, like B5 at column #8. I stacked them in their approximate locations around the edge of the floor, then Tom and I went around and laid out the bottom course for each wall. It looks as if all the pieces are here. It was a good day, though we worked for fourteen hours again.

June 18 – Took us from 7 am. till 3:30 p.m. to get all eleven vertical columns in place. We had to make sure they were level and plumb, then Tom braced them with

2-by-4s and blocking. Between 3:30 and 9 p.m. we got in five courses of timbers around all four walls. Each timber has to be slipped into the guide grooves in its adjacent columns, then it's glued along the tongue before the groove in the bottom of the timber above it is pounded down over it. Each timber is then attached to its columns with 6-inch screws at a 30-degree angle. Window and door openings call for 5-inch screws to hold one timber to another. It worked well for me to move around the cabin perimeter, gluing and pounding the timbers into place, while Tom followed behind me putting in screws with his half-inch drill powered by the gas generator. Operating the caulking gun and the adhesive that fits into it is like wielding a giant cake decorator. It's lots more fun than trying to toe nail floor joists into the foundation. I'm tired from another long day, but it's good to feel we're making progress. We cover everything with tarps at night in case it rains. Back at the float we had cups of dried noodles for supper. I was too tired to cook.

June 19 –Finished eight courses of timbers today. That brings all the walls up to ceiling height, and you can see where the windows are going to be: two each in the bedroom, kitchen, and living room, and a smaller one in the bath. The gable ends will be five courses higher, but we've run out of glue. Seems like a good stopping point for this week.

June 27 – Got to the cabin about 2 p.m. after dealing with a dead boat battery back in town. Tom has three extra days off this week, so we'll have another seven-day stint to work. I told him I want to take things a little easier this time. I don't like putting in fourteen-hour days, and

I think we need to stop for coffee breaks and lunch. I told him I want to be more conscious of the building process, but he seems to feel it's important to make lots of progress at this point. He said he'll probably feel less pressure once the roof is on and he feels the cabin and materials are protected. I'm trying to rev up my energy for one more week. Then I hope we can ease back.

With the new glue supply and plenty of screws we added all five courses of timbers for the gable walls at each end. About 6 p.m. we discovered that the timbers on opposite sides of the main column on the north wall don't match up. We've already glued everything up to ceiling height into place so we're not sure what to do. We moved on to installing headers for the windows while Tom tries to come up with a solution.

June 28 – Tom called Pan Abode through the VHF marine operator, and they said his idea for fixing the gable wall should work. He set up a guide board and recut the roofline with the skill saw. All the fooling around will probably cost us a day and a half, but Pan Abode said they'll send us a check to pay for Tom's extra work at the going construction worker's rate. We're pleased they continue to be so helpful.

June 29 – Today we cut pockets to hold the roof beams and hoisted all six of them into place. I still can't believe we did it ourselves. We dragged them from the staging area on the Wheels o' Death, hoisted them through the opening for the living room window, then lifted them up rung by rung onto step ladders at opposite ends. Tom tied them off to some bracing so they wouldn't slip down on us. The center beam was the hardest. As we tried to set it in place, we found we'd cut the pocket too small, so we had to lift it out, enlarge the pocket, then put it back again. We got all six up before we quit for the day, though.

Saw the sapsucker again today. We also watched a varied thrush foraging in the leaf litter both in the morning and the early evening. Up at the north end of the lot a winter wren sang its heart out for what seemed like half the day. I wonder if it's the same one that serenaded us last year?

July 3 – Big day today. We took down the rain shelter because we have space inside under a roof now. We also moved the barrel stove inside and set up two plastic chairs and a small wooden table I got at the thrift store in town.

I'm still flabbergasted at the incredible complexity involved in constructing a roof. We've spent the last three days laying down and fastening ceiling boards, which are a beautiful white wood—maybe pine? Each one is 6-inch-wide tongue-and-groove and 12 feet long. I counted 172 of them as I carried them across the little bridge and hoisted them up to Tom, where he stood on the ladder near the main roof beam. On top of those went a layer of heavy plastic sheeting, stapled down, then 2-by-6s every 16 inches on center at a 90-degree angle to the peak. We nailed 2-by-6 crosspieces between those. Into each of the rectangular frames those created we cut and fitted two layers of solid foam insulation. Over those (and this is just Layer 4) went 4-by-8-foot sheets of half-inch plywood. I carried the sheets of plywood from the materials pile across the stream, then slid them into a loop of rope so Tom could pull them up onto the roof.

For Layer 5 we rolled out and stapled down overlapping rows of tar paper. After that (Layer 6) we put down heavy sheets of ribbed metal roofing, 33 inches wide and 12 feet long. They will be fastened to the plywood with screws every 12 inches or so along the seams. All this will be supplemented by openings for ventilation under the eaves and special metal pieces and fastenings around the stovepipe and at the ridgeline. I guess we'll be well protected from rain, snow, and wind, but I had no idea this amount of engineering and effort would go into making that a reality.

We had dinner in front of the opening for our living- and dining-room window. What a vista we have! I'm getting used to the idea of trimming some of the trees so we can have a good view of the water and the Chilkats, even though that means the cabin will be visible to passing boats. I'm also trying to clean up the mess in the front yard from the forklift. Some of the tracks are 8 inches deep, and water has pooled up at the outflow of the stream so we have the beginnings of another marsh. I dug in a length of 4-inch plastic drainpipe in hopes the ground will firm up along the main path.

July 31 – Today wraps up another four-day work weekend. We started out by finishing the front half of "The Endless Roof." The dark green metal looks both solid and elegant, and it blends in nicely with the surrounding spruce and hemlock. The sharp peak should shed snow. Tom also put in all eight windows and the front and back doors. On Sunday we had our first fire in the barrel stove, which sits nearly dead center in the cabin and sends delicious tendrils of heat through the entire living room. Putting in insulation and siding for the interior walls has turned out to be another major

project. We had to nail vertical "furring" strips of 2-by-
3-inch lumber in the walls every 18 inches between the
support columns, then cut and fit sheets of solid foam
insulation between them. More heavy plastic sheeting
goes over that as a vapor barrier, then we can nail on the
interior siding—8-inch-wide tongue-and-groove cedar
like the exterior timbers, but only 5/8 rather than nearly
3 inches thick. Tom has devised a wooden frame to help
me cut insulation to size quickly, but it still seems this
part is taking forever.

Yesterday morning I was measuring to cut furring
strips in the bedroom. As I stood on a bucket to measure
the highest part of the wall, I was struck by the pungent,
earthy smell of warm cedar. It reminded me of the smell
in the loft in my grandparents' summer cabin back in
Rhode Island. My cousins and I used to sleep up there,
and I remember lying in my sleeping bag listening to the
grownups visiting around the big oak table downstairs. I
think lying there and looking up at the unfinished walls
and ceilings was the first time I realized buildings are
constructed of vertical and horizontal supports, of insulation and tar paper, of nails and fixtures placed at neat,
regular intervals. That cabin had been my grandfather's
dream. He built it himself with help from my uncles, and
he always insisted life should be "different" there from
life in the house in town. It had a hand pump at the sink
instead of running water, an outhouse instead of a flush
toilet, and Gramp refused against all argument to put in
more modern conveniences. I guess Tom and I are far
from the first to want the experience of doing things for
ourselves and making a place where we won't be depen-
dent on elaborate systems for our daily comforts.

August 10 – We're back out for another week, but this time we'll eat and sleep in our wonderfully enclosed, fully roofed cabin instead of on the boat. Tom has set up two big barrels and a sheet of plywood so I can arrange a camp stove and temporary kitchen. We have an air mattress and sleeping bags in the bedroom, towels and 5-gallon buckets of water in the bath. Coleman lanterns are good for lights, but we're not up long after sunset these days. We've also established systems for garbage and trash. Kitchen scraps go into the compost pile I've started against a big mossy log near the beach fringe. Burnables go into the little wood stove in Tom's shop. And we'll haul metal, recyclables, and everything else back to the dump in town.

10 p.m. - Sitting by the big living-room window, we're watching the last light fade from the sky and the water. We can see two bats flying across an opening in the trees, flashes of dark movement against the silver-gray sheen of the bay.

Tom surprised me a little after 5 o'clock today by suggesting we quit working and go for a walk. After we ate some canned stew and green beans we headed out back and through the muskeg looking for deer. It's hard to believe it's hunting season already. The muskeg was beautiful. Hundreds of little shore pines rose up above mounds of bog rosemary and Labrador tea. On the ground, shiny black crowberries and dwarf dogwood with bright red berries grew like scattered jewels in hummocks of moss, and tiny cranberries shone out here and there, ranging from lime green to almost-ripe red. On the far side of the muskeg we threaded through thick brush following the sound of water running and found a stream winding through the woods. It was a whole different world over there. The understory was lush under big old spruce and hemlock, and there were game trails down the high banks of the stream. A few tall alders with long branches stretched out sideways to reach the sun. A bear had trashed a whole section of skunk cabbage, digging up the starchy underground stems and leaving craters like Sasquatch footprints. On the walk back through the muskeg we found a perfect bear trail—alternating footsteps worn deep into the moss and leading between the cabin side of the muskeg and the stream.

August 12 – Now that the cabin walls are closed in I understand how precious light is. Suddenly all the trees I wanted to save seem to close in the house. They're in the way of either incoming light or views of the water and the woods. I can see now why some people clearcut around their houses, though it would pain me to do that here. I hope we can find a happy medium.

August 16 – What a gift! Randy, my wonderful son, and his new wife Tina want to spend three days of their honeymoon helping us work on the cabin. (They spent the first five days hiking the Chilkoot Trail.) We picked them up in *Dauntless* and had a beautiful trip out from town, then we all camped out in the cabin Monday night. Tuesday night Tom and I slept on the boat and let them have the place to themselves. Tom and Randy finished putting up the eave troughs along the front, then framed in the front deck. Tina and I cut up firewood (She's better at starting the chainsaw than I am!) and stacked it up to dry. Then both kids helped Tom put in the deck joists. I can tell already that sharing the cabin with people we love will be one of our great pleasures—though once the cabin's done we won't have to make our guests work so hard.

August 25 – Tom's dad is visiting for a few days and seems really impressed with the work we've done—though he teases that this isn't a "cabin" anymore. A cabin's supposed to have nails in the walls with greasy rags and coveralls hanging on them, he says, and you're supposed to have just pork and beans to eat and straw mattresses to sleep on. He doesn't seem to be too distraught at the improvements we've made, though, and was especially thrilled when he caught a 14-inch Dolly Varden at the mouth of the creek on the far side of the point. He and Tom have been working on the front and back decks of the cabin, while I spent most of my time painting the little toolshed and the workshop dark brown.

September 22 – Today we washed down the whole cabin with a 50 percent solution of Clorox and water, then rinsed it in preparation for staining. Tom also built steps up to the front deck on the north side next to the stream. We are seeing lots of winter wrens in the beach fringe—young ones, we think—and we caught sight of a mink running along the drift logs toward the beach.

September 23 – Tom was up early and started the wood stove—just in time, as the chill was beginning to creep under the blankets. It was even colder without him, though, so by 7:00 I could no longer lie still. A trip to the outhouse came first, but on my way I glimpsed the sun lighting up the forest on the hills across the crinkled gray water of the bay. What an invigorating sight to wake up to. The air was invigorating, too, as I'd run out in just a sweatshirt. Hope we have a bathroom indoors by winter.

rying to finish paneling inside the house.
ters for a bedroom ceiling with a storage
'll do the same above the bathroom.

ook our skiff up to the head of the bay to
with Phil and Donna and their kids Gabe
and Megan. Phil has lived here full-time for more than
twenty years and Donna for more than fifteen. Donna
homeschools both kids, who are in sixth and eighth
grades, I think. They seem to make a wonderful life here,
living a subsistence lifestyle with Phil fishing commer-
cially in the summer, and Donna maintaining their
home and growing fabulous gardens of both flowers
and vegetables. They had lots of stories about life in the
bay and the old-timers who've since passed away. Phil
says the cannery sometimes employed as many as three
hundred seasonal workers during its heyday from 1902
to 1930, and at least ten or twelve other people lived
here and fished or were retired during the 1960s, 70s,
and 80s. As a welcome gift they gave us a little book by
Lazette Ohman, who lived for twenty-one years with her
husband Gunnar in a small cabin to the east of Phil and
Donna's place.

September 24 – Last night Tom went to the outhouse
about 10 p.m., and I heard him call me through the
bedroom window. There were humpbacks feeding in the
bay. We could hear the sonorous, resonating *who. . . onk*,
sometimes two in close succession. We hurried down
to the beach and stood and listened in the dark. Heard
the blows move way up into the head of the bay. As
we stood there talking, I began to wonder if there were
any bears wandering around on the beach or on the trail
back up to the cabin, while we were down on the beach
without either a shotgun or bear spray. I think I am still

a bit spooked by the feel of the bear hide Phil showed us in his uncle's cabin last night. It was thick and furry but not really soft, and my fingers seemed to tingle as I ran them across it. Maybe the Koyukons are right—that the hide is alive even after the bear is dead. That image was still in my mind when a whale suddenly blew close in to the beach. It was so loud and all-enveloping I must have jumped a foot. Well, that's our life, or at least the life we're choosing—living among two of the biggest mammals on earth, one with an edge of real danger to it, the other less threatening but awe-inspiring in its own right. It certainly gives life a dimension I've never felt in town.

This afternoon we stained the whole exterior of the cabin. It's a beautiful honey gold color, shiny and well protected for the winter. I stained the outhouse to match, too.

September 25 – In the morning sunlight breaks from behind the cabin onto the hills across the water, then it creeps closer and starts to light up the rocks and the reef out front. Next it breaks through the big trees at the back of the cabin, and you can see it filtering down through the evergreen branches and alder leaves. Now half an hour later it's all dappled in the front yard and it perfectly lights up the path along the stream down to the beach. I can see sunlight is going to be precious here with our big trees and western exposure. Won't it be fun watching the differences in sunrise from summer to winter to spring.

9 p.m. - The bathroom's all framed in now, and we've stashed the extra trim in the storage space above the dropped ceiling for the winter.

October 5 – Yesterday Tom finished running wiring and insulating the walls in the bathroom, then we tore out the camp kitchen and insulated the south and west walls of the new kitchen. We had much discussion about where to put the lights, and what kind we should use both short-term and long-term. Propane? 12-volt DC? Or regular 110-volt AC, which we could install once we set up a battery bank and a more substantial power source. We've settled on two propane wall lamps for now, one at each end of the main living area, with two kerosene lamps and a Coleman lantern for additional light.

Here's how we know the bears were here while we were in town: There are tufts of brown hair along the edge of the deck and on the drip edge on the north side of the cabin. There's spattered mud below the living room window, and some of the unfastened deck boards have been pushed back toward the cabin wall. We found teeth marks where bears have been chewing on Jerry's cabin to the north of us, but so far they haven't shown that kind of interest here, though we were warned they might be attracted by the smell of fresh exterior stain.

October 7 – It's a great day in the morning—and at night, too. Today we installed the Sun-Mar composting toilet. There'll be no more running outside to the outhouse in the dark and cold. We now have a proper bathroom, and the outhouse will become our spare one. Tom set up a large plastic bin of peat moss, so now we just need to learn how to use the system properly. If it works as advertised, it'll be a far cry better than the outhouse. We also installed a box filled with gravel beneath the wood stove, and made a hearth out of flat rocks we gathered from the little cove northwest of the head of the bay.

October 8 – Today we finished the last of the interior furring and insulation except for three odd-shaped pieces we need to cut for the top of gable wall in the kitchen.

We spent two hours moving lumber and trim we had stacked behind the toolsheds into a stash beneath the main cabin. Two more of the original materials piles are now gone! It's hard to believe we started only six months ago with just a packing-box toolshed and a clearing for where the cabin would be.

3.

Settling In

1996

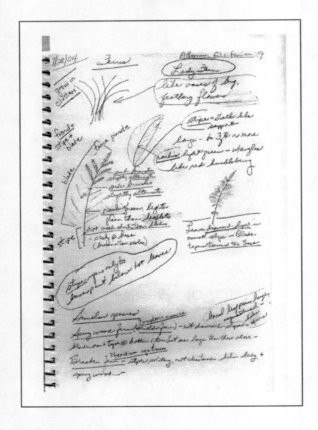

April 19 – We're leaving town aboard *Dauntless* for the first trip to the cabin since last winter. I've pulled in the fenders and secured the lines. Now, as we pull out of the harbor, I turn, as always, to watch the city's backdrop of glaciers and snow-capped mountains slide slowly into the distance. People pay thousands of dollars to come see this panorama, and Tom and I have come thousands of miles to live within it. I think I will never fail to marvel that we're making our home here.

Tom steers us through the channel, and a phalanx of green-forested islands and rocky shorelines streams past outside the wheelhouse. The water's only slightly choppy today, so there's a good chance for sighting humpback whales, sea lions, and maybe Dall porpoise. During Tom's stint at the wheel I'll fix lunch—rare roast beef on fresh sourdough buns, carrot sticks, and fresh-brewed coffee—then I'll climb up on the settee to watch the ocean and coastline unfold around us.

The 2-1/2-hour trip to the cabin nearly always generates a shift in my perceptions. With each passing mile of water we leave behind the trappings of town life: work schedules, car troubles, newscasts, grocery lists. Here we can focus on larger forces: waves and currents, forested shorelines, a sky bursting blue above white-capped peaks. We pay close attention to navigation and unpredictable weather, and we start thinking about the skills and attention we'll need to engage at the cabin.

Last summer in this same passage, we cruised within several hundred feet of six humpback whales. They swam nearly parallel with us but close in to shore. Each was longer than the full length of our boat. Six black dorsal fins and curved backs waltzed through the water—a leisurely choreography punctuated by puffs of

white moisture as each whale exhaled on rising to the
surface. I remember that incident every time we pass by
here, and the trip is richer for it. I wonder how many
more such memories we'll store up over the next thirty
or forty years?

Two hours underway, and we can see the mouth of
the bay and the craggy islands that guard the entrance.
My mariner's sense snaps to attention at the jagged
black rocks jutting out from shore and the kelp bed I
know we have to avoid along the landward shore of the
largest island. It's easy to get overly sentimental about
this country, but those rocks evoke a state of mind I've
come to associate with life in the bay: that you'd better
pay attention to what you're doing and where you mean
to go, that the threats found here are not from cars or
human beings or things of that scale, but from the larger
forces of land and sea, weather, and the large mammals
we have driven away from our cities and settled home-
sites.

Tom steers past the rocks and islands. We check for
eagles and seals and shore birds, and we watch the depth
sounder as we peer ahead for our first glimpse of the
cabin.

Today there are only a few rollers coming in from
the west, so Tom steers between the two reefs that mark
our cove and stops to anchor in front of the cabin site.
As he leaves the wheelhouse and climbs onto the bow
to drop the anchor, I take my place at the wheel, ready
at his signal to put the boat into slow reverse. This is
another time of waiting, of patience while he tests the
wind, the feel of the line, and the slow turning of the
boat to be sure the anchor is set. Then we drop into the
familiar routine: pull on rubber boots; lower the inflat-

able dinghy; fasten on the outboard and the oars; and load the first of the boxes, bags, tubs, and other gear we'll have to ferry to shore.

April 20 – We spent the first afternoon and evening just trying to settle in and get oriented again. Set up the bed, aired blankets and pillows. Set up the tabletop camp stove. Stored new groceries and took stock of the dried food we'd left in ammo boxes over the winter. Got the wood stove started. Filtered water from the rain catchment barrel and set some on the stove to heat. Set up a washing area and a bin of fresh peat moss in the bathroom. Swept the winter collection of leaves and spruce needles out of the outhouse.

We found the remains of a deer lying on the ground at the front corner of the cabin. The long vertebral column was still bloody. Two leg bones, part of the skull, and lots of fur were scattered around nearby. As we came in, Tom had spotted a mink feeding on the remains. Later we found clumps of hair and bird feathers scattered under the back deck, so we think the mink has been living, or at least feeding, there.

The cabin and its surroundings seem a bit bleak without greenery. Nothing has started sprouting, not even beach grass or skunk cabbage. The patches of blue clay on the beach are soggier than ever. Our boots sink down to the ankles nearly everywhere we step. But the stream doesn't appear to have overflowed its banks this year. Big tides washed a load of mussel shells onto the upper beach. They crunch and crackle underfoot. I'll shovel some into muddy spots on the paths around the cabin. They're a lot lighter to haul than gravel.

May 3 – There's lots of life around here today. There are new skunk cabbage shoots; and deer, I suppose, have already nibbled them right down to the ground. Throughout the day we heard crows, gulls, a woodpecker, a winter wren, and a blue grouse hooting back toward the mountain. Several pairs of Canada geese flew honking across the beach and the meadow, and two yellowlegs pattered along the water's edge at low tide. Tom found feathers of a robin apparently caught and devoured by a mink or weasel, and a hummingbird buzzed up to the front deck to check out my red jacket.

Tom finished paneling the interior front wall, both living room and kitchen. I tiled the bathroom floor and moved a supply of stove wood onto the back deck. We've pulled out the stack of building materials we had stored under the cabin so we can get into the crawl space to put in plumbing and floor insulation. We'll have copper pipes running from the rainwater storage barrels to the kitchen and bath. Tom will install a small battery-operated pump and a one-gallon pressure tank to feed the kitchen faucets. I can't wait to have running water.

May 20 – We arrived this weekend to find the northeast roof support post muddy and tufted with hair where a bear had been leaning against it and scratching. The highest mud and hair were 18 inches above Tom's head. Looks as if we have a very impressive bear in the neighborhood.

Tom got a good start on the plumbing but found he was missing several connectors he can't do without. We managed to call town and have them delivered to Ward Air in time for one of the neighbors' float plane charters. I guess we're starting to learn the ins and outs of transportation out here. Meanwhile, Tom started building a counter and medicine chest for the bathroom.

We spent several hours this weekend helping neighbors with various projects—unloading plywood and 2-by-4s and rolling a big plastic water tank into place behind one of the cabins. There are four other cabins on our side of the bay, and we've now met all the other owners. Dinners and cocktail parties: this is a part of cabin life we didn't expect.

May 29 – Tom's gone back to work, and I'm enjoying the cabin alone for a few days. This morning I finished staining the entire ceiling. I sanded the first coat of stain I'd put on Sunday and Monday, and applied the whole second coat. Then I cleaned up the mess and settled down for some quiet time. Took a folding chair down to the beach and sat in the sun to read. What a novelty! The sun was warm on my face, but I still needed my fleece pullover. Toward evening I took the inflatable out to pull the crab pot. No luck, but when I came back I saw clouds of little fish in the shallows by the outhaul. They were silvery green and about two-thirds the length of my little finger. When they'd startle and dart, all together, they made ripples and flutters and a tinkling sound. Several of them leaped out of the water in ones and twos and sparkled like fireworks, then they were gone. I wonder if they were young salmon.

June 20 – We've completed several projects in the last couple of weekends. Tom installed our new propane cook stove and oven, and built in a long plywood counter along the south wall. We have boxes beneath the counter for storing pots and pans, and plastic bins for dishes and staples. Plastic drawer units we picked up in town make good enough storage for tableware and utensils. We also made good progress on hooking up shower and sink

drains in the bathroom. Tom's using clear ribbed roofing
mounted on 2-by-4s to make skirting around the entire
base of the cabin. With that and the new floor insulation
we should be able to keep water and drains functioning
late into fall if the weather cooperates.

Tom has hooked up the CB radio and antenna, and
we're on line with the neighborhood. We've decided
to call ourselves Heron's Roost, after the big birds that
roost in the spruce trees behind the cabin. We also have
a VHF radio so we can monitor marine weather and call
out through the marine operator if necessary. The radios
are powered by two automotive batteries we can charge
with the gas generator or a solar panel once we get one
installed.

I've compiled the research I did in town on alders.
The red alders that grow around the cabin—treelike with
mottled gray and white trunks—are a different species
from the shrubby Sitka alders that predominate on the
mainland. Some of our trees have trunks bigger around
than telephone poles, but most of them curve upward at
a slant, or with odd elbows and bends. Alders are often
the first trees to colonize newly exposed ground, fertil-
izing the soil for small spruce and hemlocks that grow
up beneath them. But the spruce and hemlock outgrow
them, and the alders end up stretching at odd angles to
reach the sunlight and are eventually shaded out.

When we were clearing for the cabin we found
knobby brown growths the size of golf balls on many
of the alder roots we dug up. Apparently the knobs are
formed by filamentous bacteria that invade the alder
roots and stimulate cell growth. Those same bacteria
capture nitrogen from the air and convert it to a form
that plants can use. This fertilizes the alders and releases

nitrogen into the soil, supporting grasses, herbs, ferns, and spruce and hemlock seedlings. According to *Plants of the Pacific Northwest Coast*, compiled and edited by Jim Pojar and Andy MacKinnon, red alder stands in the Pacific Northwest can contribute up to 320 kg per hectare of nitrogen per year to their surroundings. My friend Michele, who works with scientific data, helped me translate that to about 285 pounds per acre. Not a bad contribution, even if production in Alaska doesn't match that in the warmer Pacific Northwest. Another article I found said that alder leaves are particularly high in nitrogen, so when they fall each year they contribute substantial amounts of the nutrient most lacking in the thin, wet soil around here.

I love knowing things like this. Just think—so many people say these trees grow up too fast and aren't good for much except smoking fish, but here they are actually pumping tons of fertilizer into the forests around us every year. I think they're getting a bad rap.

August 15 – What a wonderful evening we had tonight. Tom and I both sat in the living room reading our separate books, secure from a heavy rain, well fed, and warmed by the fire in the wood stove. Around us the cedar walls glowed in the soft light of the Aladdin lamp. This is what we've worked for: the quiet companionship at the end of a good day's work. We shared tea and the last of the apple crisp I'd made this afternoon while Tom was framing in an addition to double the size of his workshop.

September 2 – I'm at the cabin alone again while Tom works another ten-day shift at the plant. Donna and her daughter Megan came by, and we spent a wonderful afternoon studying plants around the cabin. After I made turkey sandwiches for lunch, we took our field guides out to the beach fringe to see how many different plants we could identify. Among the three of us we came up with at least fourteen. The cow parsnip (Indian celery) was shoulder high, and its big white umbrellalike blossoms had matured to disks of flat brownish seeds. Several western dock plants were nearly as tall, reaching as high as my waist. Their spearlike blossoms were brilliant with clusters of delicate pink flowers, and on many of the larger plants the leaves had turned a bright, almost fluorescent red.

There seem to be two kinds of angelica, one called "sea watch" or "wild celery," and a "kneeling angelica" that has leafstalks that are bent above the first pair of primary leaflets. We all knew yarrow and silverweed, bedstraw and chickweed, and I think we've identified two of the grasses as red fescue and (maybe) meadow barley. I'll have to do some more research, but it was great fun sharing what we knew and trying to come up with new i.d.'s.

September 21 – Tom and I had a bear encounter on the mine road today as we were heading home from deer hunting. I spotted the bear about the time Tom stopped short and said, "Uh-oh. Bear." It was just within sight on the road way ahead, and it was ambling straight toward us. It was medium size and very black, and it seemed to have come from the muskeg on the north side of the road. We hardly had time to think before three much smaller bears stumbled out of the brush and began milling and tumbling around the adult bear's feet. Tom yelled in a deep, loud voice, "Hup! Hup!" as if he were commanding a hunting dog, and I yelled "Hey! You get

outa here—Go on!" The bear, which we then realized
was a sow with three yearling cubs, seemed uncertain
what to do. She hesitated, batted at the cubs, then finally
turned and began walking away, still on the road, while
the cubs straggled behind. We couldn't turn off the road
and thrash through the woods, so we walked slowly after
her, keeping our distance.

After a few minutes the sow began to act uncertain
again. She turned around as if to come back up the road,
and the cubs followed her. Tom yelled again. "Hup!
Hup!" He held his rifle at the ready and checked with
me: "Do you have the safety off your bear spray?" I did,
but at that moment it seemed like small protection.

I think we were lucky the sow had all she could
manage trying to corral the three cubs. They crowded
close against her and hampered her from moving. We
were also still a good 100 yards away, so she had lots of
space for making choices. She finally turned off the road
and disappeared into the woods with the cubs following
behind.

Walking the next half-mile to where the road opens
onto the beach seemed to take forever. We walked along
slowly and deliberately, while I wondered every minute
whether an angry bear would come charging out of the
woods and blindside us. At least, I thought, it was open
enough on the road so that we would see any attack as it
was coming. I pulled the back of my coat over my head
like a hood and spread the sleeves out to the sides, trying
to look as big as I could. I also stomped with every step,
hoping to sound like a 500-pound gorilla on a rampage.
But we never saw the bear or her cubs again, and we got
back to the cabin without incident.

Later Tom and I talked about what had happened and what we might have done differently. He felt we had prevented an encounter because we were firm and clear about our intentions. He believes that here, where we are certain to come into contact with bears from time to time, it's important that we not act timid or automatically give way to them. I suppose showing strength could avert aggression between people and bears the way researchers say displays of strength often head off damaging physical encounters between bears. Well, I hope it works.

October 8 – Came in from town late and tied up *Dauntless* after dark, using the big searchlight to see the float. Left our gear to be unloaded tomorrow and headed toward the cabin in the inflatable by the light of the portable lanterns. As we pulled up to the beach we were startled by an awful screaming from the woods. All I could think of was a deer in agony, but Tom realized almost immediately it was minks squabbling. They kept it up as we came ashore and tied onto the outhaul. I couldn't help thinking of the poor little female we saw this summer all chewed up on her back end from mating. Surely they're not still mating at this time of year? Tom thought maybe it was adults chasing young ones away from home.

November 16 – Deer season. We hunted hard for two days, but no luck. Saw several small deer and one nice doe, but we never got a shot. Sunday morning I slept in and Tom went back to try a couple of promising spots we'd found earlier. At 11:30 a.m. he was back with a nice buck quartered up in his pack. We had liver with bacon and onions for dinner, and trimmed and hung the deer. We'll cut and pack it when we get back to town, where we have a vacuum packer and plastic bags to package it for the freezer.

November 17 – Had a great dinner and visit with Phil, Donna, and Megan at their place at the head of the bay. Tom wanted to walk home along the beach, but I was not keen on stumbling a mile and half across the rocks in the dark, so we accepted their offer to run us home in their skiff. Everyone came along for the ride, including their dog Polly. The stars were bright and clear, and we were treated to an unusual show of northern lights. At first they were a greenish-white glow over Juneau, then they moved steadily southward toward us till they extended across the full horizon and down to the treetops in a perfect semicircle. What an end to a dinner party!

December 6 – If we come out to the cabin again this year it will be primarily to hunt, so now seems a good time to think back over the progress we've made this year.

The cabin interior is about half finished, with paneling up and stained in the bedroom and half of the living room and kitchen. The composting toilet is set up in the bathroom, and we have cold running water and working drains for the kitchen sink, bathroom sink, and shower stall. We've drained the water system for the winter, but for now the old five-gallon buckets work fine. We heat water on the wood stove for washing dishes and to fill the garden sprayer we use to take showers. The temporary kitchen is stocked, and I can now bake bread and biscuits in the oven of the new propane range.

We've finished installing vinyl tile flooring throughout cabin, and we've set up a futon in the living room for a couch and fold-out guest bed. The barrel stove is ensconced in a temporary hearth with wood box, and now that there's floor insulation and skirting around the whole base of the cabin we're warm all night long.

Outdoors we've cleared more stumps and brush and laid flat stones and slabs from the stumps to improve several of the paths. I also trimmed a few more branches to improve the water and mountain view. Not bad for a season's work.

4.

Life in the Woods

1998-2001

Rattlesnake Plantain
10-5-06

1998

April 6 – We arrived Friday to open the cabin for the season. Everything survived the winter except that we'd had some animal visitors. A mouse got into the kitchen and shredded an entire roll of paper towels. I found its nest—empty—in the silverware box and mouse droppings all over the counter. Had to wash everything. We think the mouse got in through the hole in the floor where the copper tubing comes up to connect the new cook stove to the propane tanks under the cabin. Tom made a tin cover to seal off the hole, and he made an Alaskan mousetrap out of a five-gallon bucket for under the house.

But there was worse news. We noticed an awful stench around the outside of the cabin, and when we checked around to investigate we found that a mink had wintered under the cabin in the crawl space. It had dragged in several salmon carcasses, and remnants of them were still there, half eaten and rotting away into slime. Together with the mink's fetid droppings they made a disgusting mess. It took us several hours to shovel it out and dispose of the smelly dirt. Later Tom will put some chicken wire and rocks beneath the skirting to try to keep critters out in the future.

Getting ready to start the year is a somewhat bigger project these days. As I swept floors and took inventory of groceries on hand and supplies we need, Tom reconnected the water system, cleaned cobwebs out of the toilet vent fan, and restocked the peat moss bin. For outdoor exercise we cut up a big alder that looked ready to fall toward the cabin, then bucked up and stacked the wood.

We're also frantically preparing for Tom's weekend off at the end of the month, because we've scheduled another delivery by the landing craft. This time it will bring out a large excavator we're renting to help install the wind generator pole, the 3-kilowatt Lister diesel generator we bought secondhand in town, and more building materials. We've rented the excavator for only three days; then it's scheduled at another site in the bay, so we'll need to accomplish a lot in a short time. To prepare, we're moving a few more rocks off the beach, clearing temporary places for the generator and building materials to sit, and assembling the hardware for raising the pole. We've leveled a site for a small shed to house the new generator, and Tom has put in foundation posts, but he won't have materials to build the shed till they arrive on the landing craft.

Despite being so busy we're enjoying the first signs of spring. The beach grass is showing green shoots, one bright yellow skunk cabbage is poking up a good three inches out of the mud, and leaves are starting to open on the elder bush. Chickadees and juncos are flocking through the beach fringe, there's a flock of robins working the beach meadow, and there are harlequins and buffleheads feeding in the water out front.

April 24 – I flew in alone yesterday with Ward Air, three days before Tom is due in on the landing craft. Settling in is not as much fun alone as it is with Tom, but by bedtime the place had warmed up, and even the sheets had lost their chill.

I spent most of this morning watching two Canada geese feeding on the beach meadow right out front. They sure are striking birds, with their brown plump bodies and brilliant white chin straps. When they flew in, they landed down at the water's edge, which surprised me because they had to patter across the low-tide mud and rocks to get up to the grass. I thought rough ground would bother their feet, which look so broad and floppy, but they seemed to have no problem with it. They just padded along, peering about and stopping to eat long streamers of yellow-green sea lettuce that had washed up on the beach. Eventually they moved up into the beach grass (it's actually sedge, I think), which is showing several inches of green shoots now. When I went down there after they'd left, I could see the grass was bitten down to about an inch above ground level.

It's a slow, deliberate process, sinking into soli-tude—a process I'm learning to relish. It's thick, like being submerged in clumps of wool. I'm deliberately slowing my blood flow, decelerating my mind and body from the busy, exciting pace of town life. Here on the couch, watching muted sunlight shift and glimmer over the bay, all I hear is the intermittent crackle of the fire, and a burbling as the red enamel coffeepot starts to boil. First come a series of slow pops, then the steady rhythm of water tumbling over and over upon itself. For so much of my life gentle quiet like this was always tinged with a painful yearning. I wanted solitude in association with a loving relationship. Now Tom and I have that, and I feel content and immensely grateful.

April 25 – 12:30 p.m. – A lovely 17.8-foot high tide. I put on my chest waders and went down to the beach to maneuver the wind generator pole from where we had anchored it on Tom's last weekend off. We bought the brand-new pole from the local electrical utility and had it delivered to the harbor in town; then we towed it out to the cabin behind *Dauntless*. After hauling a whole raft of poles out here, as we did a few years ago, dragging a single one was easy, even though it's 68 feet long and weighs a couple thousand pounds. It's floating up the beach fairly nicely now, and I've maneuvered it so the base is pointing directly at the place where Tom said he wants to seat it. Tomorrow morning, when the tide is higher, I'll go out and move the anchor closer yet, and I'll see if I can get it all the way up the beach by Tuesday.

April 28 – Tom's due in this afternoon on the landing craft. My farthest-out pole, marking where the big rock sticks up, is underwater at high tide. Well, if the water is that deep, they won't need to worry about the rock, but if they come early perhaps it will steer them away from it.

May 1 – The wind generator pole is up and securely planted. What a project! It took us from 6 a.m. to 9 p.m. on Wednesday to get it right. Tom used the excavator to dig a hole 8 feet deep, then he attached guy wires on three sides of the pole for bracing. He used the excavator arm and bucket to move the gigantic thing over the hole, dangling it from a sling, then gradually pushed and pulled to tip it upright and into position. We ended up having to set it three times. The first time the cable holder on one guy wire let go as we were tightening it, so we had to lower the pole and refasten the hardware. Then after we'd tipped the pole upright again, one guy wire had tangled around the hoist strap and we had to let it down. Finally we got the thing upright again, then it was check, adjust, check, and adjust several more times before we were sure the pole was standing up straight. Packing the ground back around the base of the pole would have been easier if we hadn't run into blue clay. The darn stuff stuck to the excavator bucket in big, gluey clumps, so half the time we had to scrape it off with shovels and heave it into the hole by hand. How could we have done this without Tom's history of working with heavy equipment and his experience handling structures like this utility pole? This is a bigger project than I'd expected just to set up a system to generate our own wind power.

Tom spent the rest of our equipment rental time pulling rocks to the side to clear a broader swath of beach along the outhaul, and digging a 60-foot trench to extend the gray-water line that drains the kitchen and bathroom sinks and the shower. We moved the Lister and building materials close to where the generator shed will be and wrapped them with tarps against the weather.

May 3 – I've worked hard the past couple of days trying to clean up the destruction wreaked by the excavator. I spent one morning hauling more rocks away from the outhaul and filling in the track from the top of the beach to the generator shed. I did some more grading around the pole and planted several small spruce trees. Meanwhile, Tom worked long hours on the generator shed. He finished the floor and walls last night and skidded the Lister in along two planks, using a come-along. This morning I helped him nail on all the plywood siding. This afternoon while I loafed and let my right (hammering) arm recover, he finished installing the roof. I guess we'll be free now to spend Tom's next weekend working on the cabin—sheet-rocking the east kitchen wall and installing the cabinets we ordered from Seattle.

May 16 – We got to watch two bears on our beach this morning. They were both small, I'd guess two-and-a-half-year-olds. They meandered along the beach, stopping only to munch grass. They seemed oblivious to us and the cabin.

June 20 – There's lots of social activity in the bay these days. All the owners are here in the five cabins around us, and we've all had family or friends visiting for various periods of time. The CB radio carries a steady stream of invitations for cocktails or dinner or the offer of occasional help with a big project. I'm surprised I enjoy being part of a small, informal community like this, and I'm fascinated by our conversations when we get together. Someone always has a problem to solve with a generator, or an idea for a new kind of hot-water heater, or a good bear story from the past week or the old days when so many characters lived out here. We learn from each other and do a lot of problem-solving over tea or cocktails. What's the best way to install a solar panel? What did you use to catch that halibut yesterday? What would you have done if you'd run into that sow with the two yearling cubs on the way over here? Somehow it seems more important than a lot of the conversations we have in town.

July 12 – Well, there's controversy brewing in the bay. A couple of commercial crabbing boats have been putting huge numbers of pots in the bay. A number of them are crowding the places where some of us traditionally put our personal-use pots, and they're difficult to maneuver around on the water, too. Some cabin owners want to petition to close the bay to commercial crabbing; others believe the crabbers are locals who are trying to make a living, while many cabin owners are seasonal visitors who come for recreation then leave and make their livings elsewhere. I admit the number of pots this year seems excessive, but if we shut out local food harvesting, what will people do for a living? Not everyone in Southeast Alaska can work for a box store or a private company or government agency, and some folks don't want to. Some want to live off the land, as Tom and I hope to do, whether gathering their own food or harvesting to sell to others. Tom says it's odd that so many of us come out here to get away from regulations, then once we get here we want to bring all the regulations with us to protect what we want to do. It's a thorny issue—the difficulty of sharing common resources that people seem to be struggling with all over the world.

Oct. 16 – A brisk wind is blowing from the north today, and the wind generator is spinning nicely. I'm glad Tom had experience climbing power poles in Michigan, and that he had a proper safety belt as he made his way up and down those spike steps. It was nerve-wracking to see him up there at the top, but he built a platform so he can work up there, then mounted the wind generator on long metal pipes bolted to the top of the pole. The pipes telescope so he can drop the generator down to work on it, then raise it up when it's ready to go to work.

We dug a trench and buried a cable from the base of the pole to the battery system under the cabin. Now the meter Tom installed in the living room next to the radios shows the batteries charging up with not a drop of gasoline or diesel burned. With both wind power and the new solar panel, we should be able to reduce our dependence on hauling fuel from town and be a little more environmentally friendly, too.

Nov. 26 – Thanksgiving week at the cabin. What pleasures! I now have a "real" kitchen with blond maple Shaker-style cabinets and a stainless steel counter and sink. We have a small refrigerator and freezer now, too, and it has a great history. Our neighbors Bill and Helen were planning to throw it away because two bears tore into it when they broke into Bill and Helen's cabin several years ago. But Tom replaced the burner in the propane cooling system, and I was able to scrub the whole thing down so it looks and smells quite presentable. We've given the whole neighborhood a good laugh with our "refrigerator that the bears trashed," but I for one am delighted to retire the small propane and picnic coolers we'd been using till now.

1999

April 2 – First time we've seen the cabin in snow. We had to shovel so we could walk through a big drift between the cabin and the outhouse. There's another big drift over the bridge and en route to the lumber pile, but the rest of the yard is clear. You can see that the northerlies must howl through here in the winter. Still, there are signs of spring. There were geese on the beach when we pulled in, though I think they'll be hard pressed to find many green sprouts. Half a dozen robins worked clear patches in the yard this afternoon. And I heard a winter wren singing just once.

We hiked out back to the muskeg to see how much snow was left there. On the way we saw some rattlesnake plantain plants dug up and lying with their roots exposed. Did a deer eat the evergreen leaves? That would be new to me. I've never seen rattlesnake plantain listed as deer food.

There were lots of snowdrifts left in the muskeg, too, some of them calf-deep when we stepped in them. Yet there are also patches completely clear with moss exposed. The moss looks worn, as if it hasn't had time to revive, so maybe it's only recently emerged. As we approached the cabin on the way back, we saw a mink running through the woods toward the beach.

April 3 – Today we're digging in the crawl space under the cabin to make room to install two 55-gallon water storage barrels laid on their sides. We've cleared 6 to 8 inches of dirt from a space about 4 feet by 12 feet by 3 feet. Phil came by just as Tom was using the come-along to drag out a huge boulder we ran into. "You're supposed to do that before you put up the cabin," he laughed. "Yeh, we know that now," Tom said.

April 4 – Today is Easter and the start of Daylight Savings Time. I see no signs of buds popping on the trees or brush, no bright green tips on the spruce or hemlock branches, not a sign of ferns leafing out. Only the moss along the stream is bright green and healthy looking. It's mounded in soft green cushions with little hairlike stems and spore caps coming out of it. The stream is quite full, and it makes beautiful little waterfalls over the rocks before it flattens down and skims over the bedrock just below the bridge. The bedrock is marble like the reef out front, and it glows white and gold beneath the inch or two of water flowing over it.

June 1 – We planted potatoes and lettuce this afternoon in three cut-off barrels out on the beach. I hope the plants do as well as they did last year. The weather cleared yesterday, and at last it's beginning to feel as though summer might come. It feels so good to be working outside without rain!

June 5 – Tom's gone back to work, and I'm at the cabin on my own again. I went up-bay exploring this afternoon in our new secondhand aluminum skiff. It's roomier and faster than the inflatable, and I enjoy being able to travel farther afield. On the beach at the head of the bay I saw a gaunt-looking sow with two roly-poly cubs of the year. The cubs were cute, gamboling around like large puppies. The sow has strange markings. She's dark overall with a big swath of golden brown across her hips and haunch.

June 6 – This afternoon I went with Phil, Donna, and their kids on a skiff expedition several miles south of the bay. We walked along two beautiful streams near an old fish camp, and explored tidepools on the beach. Saw some gorgeous yellow flowers clustered in crevices among the rocks on the cliffs and wondered what they were. When I got home I found them in Pojar and MacKinnon. They're villous ("hairy") cinquefoil (*Potentilla villosa*) and are closely related to the silverweed that grows thick on our beach. They have beautiful rose-like yellow blossoms with orange lines radiating out from a cluster of stamens in the center. Their leaves look almost identical to wild strawberry leaves. I also took notes on another flower we saw in the same environment. It was very small, a white flower the size of my smallest fingernail that opened into a delicate pinkish-white star. The flower grew at the top of a single, fine stem and had five or more slender, oval leaves all coming up from the base. The leaves were dark green with a reddish cast to them. Pojar and MacKinnon say they're northern star flower (*Trientalis arctica*). That seems an appropriate name for such a lovely little plant.

I keep hearing birds calling when I go out on the front deck of the cabin, and I've decided they must be marbled murrelets out on the water. I could see three dark spots out there this afternoon and distinctly heard their peeps—very high-pitched and sometimes breaking into two syllables, like *whee-er, whee-er*. The birds are at least a quarter mile from the beach, so the sound must be carrying a long distance over the water. I've always enjoyed watching murrelets from the boat. They seem so plucky and energetic, like little brown high-powered torpedos. What fun to hear them from the cabin and imagine them out there diving down and scarfing up little fish.

June 8 – Two bears appeared on our beach about 8 a.m. this morning, and I figured out afterward they must have been the amorous pair folks have been talking about seeing for the last week. I saw the first one in the grass on our side of the little pond. "She"(?) was just munching like a peaceful cow. When she turned abruptly aboutface and walked steadily across the meadow to the foot of our stream, I thought she was moving away from a skiff going by out front. But soon a second bear popped up near where she'd first been and followed nearly in her footsteps. As they came close together they moved behind the big rock at the base of our path, and I couldn't see their interaction. But seconds later the second bear ("He"?) came walking back across the top of the beach the way he'd come. Then he stopped, looked back, and woofed six or seven times as if asking "Her" to follow him. It was the strangest sound—something like a deep grunt but higher pitched so it sounded like something between a grunt and a bark. Apparently the lady declined because she kept moving slowly north, and he turned around and kept heading south.

Seeing something like this adds so much to my life and my appreciation for where we are. It's a simple thing, and so easily missed. You just have to be in the right place at the right time. It makes me think about what I learned about just "being around" when I was single-parenting and Randy was growing up. In spite of scheduled plans to do things together, some of our unplanned encounters turned out to be the times of greatest connection—and they wouldn't have happened if I hadn't been just hanging around. I guess that's a lot like what Tom and I are doing by living out here— hanging around in a setting where we hope meaningful encounters and observations will occur. We can't dictate that neat things will happen, but we can sure try to be around to catch some of the high points.

June 30 – I'm at the cabin alone again, hoping to get some writing done on a couple of articles for the *Alaskan Southeaster*. Last night just after midnight I heard a bear close to the cabin. From the bathroom I could hear the rhythmic "plunk" of footsteps as it walked around the back. It seemed to go back and forth along the corner as if it was sniffing the building. Then I heard the clicking of its teeth. It was too dark to see it out the window. Then the noise seemed to get louder, and I wondered if it was not a bear at all but a squirrel gnawing on the foundation boards. I pounded hard and fast on the bin of the composting toilet, and the metal frame resounded like a bass drum. There was a noise as of footsteps running away, then almost immediately the footsteps began again. I listened hard till I recognized the sound of rain dripping off the trees onto the big devil's club leaves along the stream. Went back to bed feeling pretty foolish.

July 21 – Tom worked all day installing a new 2500-watt inverter that will convert DC power from the batteries to AC power for lights inside the cabin. It will mean we can store up power from the solar panels and wind generator in the batteries, then draw on it through the inverter. If solar and wind fail, we can also charge the batteries or run lights directly off the diesel generator. A 2500-watt inverter is larger than we need for lights and power tools, but that's the smallest inverter Tom could find that has a true sine wave so we'll have reliable voltage levels when I bring my laptop computer and printer out here so I can write. Now Tom has to move the batteries to the workshop and run a cable from there. Under the cabin, as they were, they were too exposed to weather and condensation. We talked about trying to get an internet connection out here someday, but it would have to be by satellite, and we don't have a clear sight line at the right angle. We wonder, too, if it would just add a lot of stress trying to keep a system going out here with all the inevitable glitches. Maybe more importantly, how much would that connection cut into the peace and solitude we cherish so much here?

October 2 – Heard ravens making a racket in the trees around the cabin when we arrived yesterday. They were cawing and flying around, making that watery, gurgling noise that sounds so odd. Then I heard one calling from a tree, and it sounded just like a songbird. It put out such high-pitched singing and warbling I thought at first I was hearing some other kind of bird. But the sound was too regular, and it was in duet with the usual raven caws and croaks. When we hiked back to the muskeg about 3 p.m. to hunt, I got to watch another raven (or was it the same one?) perched in a shore pine. I could see it open its beak and see its throat bulge as the warbling sound issued forth. The noise was distinctly unravenlike. Was it some kind of courting call?

We soon realized there was a huge flock of ravens out there. I counted maybe twenty of them right around us at a single time. Tom thought there were about fifty altogether. They were flapping back and forth over the muskeg and flying overhead in circles. All I could think of was a bunch of kids at a carnival riding around in bumper cars, except that the birds moved smoothly and never crashed together. Sometimes they flew really high, soaring out toward the bay and back toward the woods. At times we'd see a pair flying in tandem, swerving under and above each other, doing barrel rolls, and flying straight ahead. Sometimes three or more perched in a tree and just watched what the others were doing. All the while the birds were cawing and squawking in typical raven fashion, and occasionally we'd hear that songbirdlike melody. Today I can still hear them cawing, still out back in the muskeg, I suppose. I wonder if this is a seasonal gathering for choosing mates or something? Will all these birds stay flocked up for the winter? Is there a dominant pair—maybe the ones whose territory this is during summer?

November 25 – Thanksgiving Day – Tom and I left early to hunt after a breakfast of ten-grain pancakes. There sure are a lot of buck rubs in the muskeg. A couple of small shore pines have been almost completely debarked. All their branches are broken off, and the stringy light tan inner bark is showing. Some of the larger ones have foot-long gouges on a 4-inch swath of bark. Those poor little trees are on such a tight margin to survive. I wonder how wear and tear like this affects them over the long term?

We hiked several miles, meandering through the woods to the head of the bay, but no luck, so we walked home along the beach rocks. I was pretty tired when we got back, but enjoyed preparing Thanksgiving dinner. I made pumpkin squares, then put the turkey roll in the oven to cook for two and a half hours. Our menu also included fresh yams covered with pineapple juice, brown sugar, and butter; dressing with cranberries, bacon, and onion; mashed potatoes from the garden; cranberry sauce; and a romaine salad. After a wonderful, relaxing evening we decided we have a lot to be thankful for.

November 27 – This morning we left the cabin right after breakfast to hike over by the mine road in search of deer. I misunderstood Tom and thought we were going on a loop up to the alpine, where I got my little deer last year. Instead he meant a loop over toward the avalanche slide, where he got the big buck earlier this fall. I was glad we'd stayed together instead of separating and ending up waiting at two different ends of the woods.

We had barely approached the slide, climbing up fairly high on the hillside, when Tom stopped short and motioned me to stop. Almost immediately he shot, and we had another deer. It was a lovely forked buck with just the first tines of antlers. It was hard to see such a beautiful animal die, but at least Tom got it with a solid head shot. Tom skinned and quartered it while I kept watch for bears, then we carried it back to the cabin in the Alaskan frame pack.

November 28 – A very satisfying day cutting up the deer. We had great fun watching the ravens, magpies, and Steller's jays come to take the scraps we put out on an alder stump by the kitchen window. The magpies are so beautiful. Their plumage is sleek and startling, the purple sheen of their black feathers contrasting with the snowy white of their bellies and wing patches. The two ravens were cleverer, though. They were reluctant to come to the stump to take scraps, so they just perched in a nearby tree and waited till the magpies picked some up; then they chased the magpies till they dropped the scraps, and swept in and took them.

2001

April 15 – This morning I watched two red-breasted sapsuckers circling the snag behind the cabin. Eventually one began tapping a hole—I think the male, from what I've read. He seemed the one most focused on the job, while what I think was the female landed beside him only once, then hung around close by, flitting among other trees, landing on the trunks, and pecking.

April 17 – Watched the sapsucker at his hole again. He is amazing. He stabs his beak against the tree—fast-fast-fast like a jackhammer tapping. His head is a blur, but I can see the chips flying as he works. He's made a roundish hole about 3 or 4 inches in diameter in the bark. Won't it be great if he and his mate build a nest here?

April 18 – **9:30 a.m.** - The sapsucker is pecking at his hole again. He's through to a light-colored layer now. You can see a pale ring around the inside edge of the hole, and beyond that a dark layer—the heartwood? The female stays close by, flying about from tree to tree. Later as I watched the male I heard her call—that mewling chirp sapsuckers make. He stopped chipping and just sat there – getting instructions?

April 21 –All I wanted to do this morning was sit on the front deck and read in the sun. I'd barely gotten started when a squall come through from the southeast. I first heard it coming when the wind chime on the back deck began tinkling, then gradually clattering louder and wilder. Next the wind in the trees got louder, and the tops of the big spruce and hemlock started thrashing. The noise was so loud I wondered if I was hearing surf hitting the cliffs near the mouth of the bay. Just as the rain came pelting down, I slid my chair beneath the roof overhang. I sat with the same excitement and fluttering stomach that I remember having when as a kid I sat out storms on our covered front porch in southeastern Massachusetts. Back there the best rain came with thunderstorms, too. But that porch was screened all around and sheltered by a covey of overhanging maple trees. I sat many a summer's day on the saggy old couch out there with a stack of books beside me, reading to the sound of rain and thunder, and smelling the sharp, electric tang in the air. Out here there are no pyrotechnics, but I can see across low-lying land and water for miles. I watch the bay crinkle with ripples, then dark waves, and I feel a little shiver of fear as whitecaps flash their gleaming teeth out in the channel. I imagine rain beating onto the outer coast of Southeast Alaska, then plunging into the inland waterways like a flood-swollen river. It roars up the watery corridors and into every space between islands and the mainland till it reaches us here, in this small outpost on the long Inside Passage. Imagine being able to experience all that, then in a few steps walk indoors and settle into a cozy recliner with a bowl of hot soup. I thank my lucky stars and so many people along the way that I can be here like this.

April 22 – Relaxing after lunch at the dining room window and watching robins feed. Six or eight of them are fanned out across the front yard, moving on little stick legs with stop-start runs and hops. Every few paces they stop and poke into the ground with their beaks, tossing leaves aside and I suppose picking up insects or worms. Later a single varied thrush runs among them, hardly distinguishable except for its different plumage. Run-run-run. Stop. Stand still (Are they listening then?). Run now in a different direction, flashing dark brown heads, yellow beaks, and brick-red breasts. I can see the white streaks under their chins. What pretty birds they are, and how often do we say, "Oh, it's just a robin."

June 9 – Tom is working on a pole barn addition to the generator shed. He's cut eight small spruce and hemlock trees for uprights and is cutting 2-by-4s from some big spruce boards he sliced out with his chain saw sawmill summer before last. Soon we'll have more room to store tools and a space where we can work out of the rain.

Have seen no sign of the sapsuckers this trip. I'll feel really sorry if all our activity frightened them away from a good nest site.

July 22 – Yesterday was jam-packed with the good things I love about being out here. Had an early quiet breakfast with Tom. Chatted about interesting things, including the book he is reading—Stephen Ambrose's account of the Lewis and Clark expedition. As he went out to work on the pole barn, I went to the north end of the lot to take out part of an old stump and some overgrown slash. I want to make a trail so we can walk to this area from the back door of the cabin, across the little stream.

I hacked dirt from around the big root arms of the stump. The trunk is a full 2 feet across at my waist height and has moss and little plants growing in its rotting top.

As I cleared the root arms I found they had grown down over the top of another cut-off stump! So this land has been logged at least three times. The top stump is bigger and obviously years older than the less-rotted logs lying around from the cut in the 1950s. The stump beneath it was big, too—maybe sixty or seventy years old. So that's three growths of trees on this same ground. I think the earlier cuttings must date back to the early 1900s, when the mine and the cannery were operating full-time.

I love making these discoveries and, maybe more so, rooting around in the dirt. Working in the earth that way is so satisfying. I want to shape it gently and pay attention to what's happening. Things go pretty slowly when you use a mattock, loppers, a scratcher, and then the chain saw, but it keeps me aware of what I am changing—hopefully without dire effects—and, who knows, maybe in a way helpful to some birds or plants. Now that I'm done, the stump is still sitting there, nursing the little seedlings on its top, but we can walk past it on a path about three feet wide to the other end of the lot. I saved the best patches of moss from the ground I disturbed and replanted them, hoping they'll spread over some patches of bare ground. I also moved the pile of bathroom compost. Made a bin to contain it with rotten logs I had stacked elsewhere from other clearing. If it breaks down as it's supposed to, we'll have a good supply of soil to go around the blueberry bushes in a few years.

It was an overcast day, but warm and not raining, so Tom and I enjoyed a coffee break down on the beach, with lemon-blueberry muffins I made during a break from clearing. We saw birds all day long: herons on the beach, juncos (including a small one following an adult and being fed), two young-looking winter wrens. Heard a woodpecker in the alders above me.

At 6 p.m. Donna and Megan picked us up and took us in their skiff for a picnic on one of the small islands at the mouth of the bay. We squeaked into the beach through thick kelp just before a very low tide. Built a bonfire of driftwood and cooked hot dogs, beans, and s'mores.

Megan and I explored tidepools on the in-bay side of the island. They were full of life. The barnacles out there are as big as my thumb to the first joint. Some of them were completely covered with a pink crustose algae that had extended from patches on the rocks and flowed right over them. Besides the usual black periwinkles there were hundreds of pinkish-orange conch-shaped ones. A third type was pearly white and almost translucent like parchment, with crenelations an eighth of an inch or more deep. I found in Rita and Charles O'Clair's *Southeast Alaska's Rocky Shores: Animals* that the pink ones are called wrinkled amphissa (*Amphissa columbiana*). Not sure about the white ones. We also saw sea urchins, some quarter-size and others with their spines open and as large across as my outstretched hand; chitons with black and white stripes and as big as my thumb to the first knuckle, too; groups of small limpets the size of the nail on my ring finger; and what the O'Clairs call "Christmas anemones" (*Urticina crassicornis*)—leathery knobs, olive-green with red splotches and with whorls of blunt-tipped tentacles; they apparently feed on chitons, crabs, sea urchins, mussels, and little fish. Huge patches of rocks were crowded with mussels. Looking at the ones underwater we could see the mussel shells were partly open and the "lips" around the rims were feeding with tiny tentacles extended. I told Megan I wanted to see a gunnel, and she overturned some rocks and found several small ones 3 to 4 inches long. They are dark squiggly little fish, like the ones I have been watching the herons catch on our beach. One, dark brown, had strings of light brown spots down its side.

Megan and I climbed up the rock bluff to the center of the island and explored under the big spruce and hemlock trees that seem to flourish there. Beneath them we found thick brush of alder, blueberries, and currants. Beard lichens hung so thick in places I wondered how the trees could breathe. We found deer and fish bones, and two 4-inch-long gumboot chiton shells that I packed up and carried home. Donna gave me a great piece of driftwood she found that's shaped just like a raven's head, with a hole for the left eye and tufts of seaweed hanging down like the decorations on a Tlingit mask. I'll mount it in a place of honor in one of my gardens. In the upper level of rocks, where soil had collected, we found yellow paintbrush growing among the grasses and lupine. I've not seen it growing anywhere on the big island.

Sixty degrees and still light when we came home at 9:45 p.m. Tom saw a mink run along the drift log as we tied up the skiff. What a day for sightings!

November 15 – Another great wildlife sighting to begin my week alone at the cabin. I had just finished lunch and was beginning to unpack when my attention was caught by what looked to be a dark brown sparrow fluttering back and forth just outside the kitchen window. I went to the bedroom window to look more closely from the side. No wonder the fluttering wings had looked so odd. I wasn't seeing a bird—it was a bat! It was swooping back and forth across the south end of the cabin. Back and forth it went, again and again, sweeping high, dropping low, but always turning and flying 25 to 30 feet across the end of the house.

Now and then it disappeared for a moment—maybe circling around the back corner of the house? But soon it was back. This was the closest I'd ever been to a bat, and I was fascinated by its odd-shaped wings and prominent Mickey Mouse ears.

Was it feeding on a hatch of bugs, even this late in the year? Why was it flying around so early in the day? It was barely 2 o'clock, and till now I'd only seen bats flying around near dusk. Was this one out early because the day was so drizzly and overcast?

I watched the bat perform its loops, wondering how long it would follow this same pattern and stay in one place. Eight minutes passed (I estimated the start of the sighting and began timing out of curiosity). Then suddenly—*whooomph!*—I saw a flash of dark feathers with white spots, and a long grayish barred tail. A hawk had collided with the bat in midair and flown off with it!

I ran to the door and peeked behind the cabin. Yes, there was movement—a whitish flash dipped up and down, up and down, from over on a big, moss-covered log beyond the woodpile. The hawk was eating. I ran back to the desk for my binoculars so I could watch. The hawk took ten minutes to consume its prey. Its head moved up and down again and again. I imagined a fierce beak tearing at tough skin to reach the soft flesh and wondered who to feel sorry for—the bat, or the bird that would need all the energy it got from its meal to survive a long winter. I could see nothing of the bat, except that at one point the hawk lifted its beak and stretched out something wide and brown that I feel certain was a wing. That seemed odd. Can there be anything edible on a wing? Maybe there was, because the hawk tore at it persistently for several minutes.

Through the binoculars I tried to see more of the hawk, though I stayed on the deck close to the cabin wall so I wouldn't frighten it away from its meal. What kind was it? It was bigger than a robin but much smaller than a raven. It had a cream-colored breast with heavy brown streaking. Its body feathers looked dark brown and had numerous distinct white spots. Its tail was long and lighter colored than the body, with four or more dark bars across it.

Finally the hawk flew away, low and parallel to the ground, and I lost sight of it among the big trees behind the beach fringe.

I walked over to the log, thinking I might find remnants of the bat—a skull or a wing maybe, something inedible. But there was not a trace. If I had not seen the incident I'd never have known it had happened.

I checked my field guides and think the hawk might have been an immature sharp-shinned, but it's hard to reconcile what I saw with the descriptions and photos. Not that it really matters. What I remember most is how the bat's wings fluttered when it flew. It seemed such an odd movement—like the flapping of a wounded bird. The wings seemed to fold and undulate rather than flap as a single piece the way birds' wings do. It's certainly distinctive, and for some reason it made me feel uneasy. Is that some sort of primitive response, or did I read too many Halloween stories when I was a kid?

It seems kind of foolish that the bat kept flying back and forth in such a steady pattern across the end of the house. Was there a cloud of insects clustered there beneath the overhang of the roof? Maybe the bat was reveling in a great burst of food. But even when they're feasting, don't most animals instinctively shy away from repetitious, predictable motion because it makes them more vulnerable to predators? And how did the hawk see it, so close to the house, where the building would block the view from all but a small part of the woods? Did the hawk just happen to be cruising by, or was it perched in the beach fringe, waiting for the sight of a deer mouse or a vole?

November 16 – This morning I called Bob Armstrong on the cell phone. He couldn't tell for sure from my description, but he wondered if the "hawk" might rather have been a merlin (a falcon), which might be more adept at capturing an animal in flight. He said an immature one would be about the same size as a sharp-shinned hawk and could have very similar plumage to what I saw. I'll never know, I guess; but that doesn't detract from the excitement of having seen the actual encounter.

November 17 – I've looked for the telltale flitting shadows the last two evenings, but there are none. Are all our bats gone? When will others move in to take their place?

November 19 – The wind has been fierce from the north since yesterday afternoon; in fact, the roar of the wind generator kept me awake much of the night. High tide came up past the outhaul posts, carrying lots of seaweed that I'm hauling up the beach for the compost pile. During some of yesterday's worst gusts I watched a pair of harlequin ducks standing on a rock just beyond the reef. They faced right into the wind, and didn't budge. Do they love just standing there as the waves splash water up and over their chests and heads? The big flock of goldeneyes I saw before the wind hit must have taken shelter up at the head of the bay. They travel in much larger groups than the harlequins, never seem to climb out onto land, and disappear into the lee when the wind comes up.

November 20 – There's less wind today, but Tom still flew in a little early because the forecast is for more foul weather. I was ready in my chest waders to help ferry baggage and hold the plane off the beach. The pilot told Tom he has me well trained. Ha!

November 21 – We've decided we need more indoor space, so we're planning an addition to the cabin. It will be 16x20 feet, and will house a workspace where I can have a desk and bookshelves for my work, a small captain's bed for guests, and a small bath with a composting toilet, and a wash basin with a simple foot-pump water supply. We don't want to cut into the main cabin roof and walls, so the addition will be a separate building. It will sit at an angle that causes the least interference with the view from the windows of the main cabin, and will look, from the front window, over the beach meadow and pond, and to the side into the path through the big spruces that I call Cathedral Walk. We'll order a Pan Abode package again, since that worked so well last time. Tom will finalize our plans and order the package this winter. We'll handle the foundation up to floor level ourselves again, so he's already begun dinging post holes. Earlier this month he was out there digging in the midst of a snowfall. He wants to make progress before the ground freezes.

December 23 – I'm sitting on the rocky ledge just north of our beach. I can look 180 degrees and see the whole bay from here. It's agreed—we're going to buy this small piece of land to the north of the cabin and the lot to the south. Now we'll own the grove of trees that protects the cabin from northerlies, and we should have plenty of privacy if more cabins go in on either side of us. I hope we've made a good decision. We're committed to this place for the long term now.

We did our initial clearing with hand tools and a chain saw.
From left, Lucy, John, Tom, with Pops cranking on the
comealong, far right.

The outhaul gives us access to our skiff and dinghy even
though our local tides vary by more than 20 feet.

Tom and I took different approaches to digging foundation post holes.

Tom floating the first raft of foundation poles in Auke Bay harbor.

I couldn't believe it took $345-worth of materials to build an outhouse.

First course of walls going up on the original cabin.

The cabin looks out onto the beach meadow and a small pond. Beyond that we see the mouth of the bay with the snow-tipped Chilkat Mts. in the distance.

Ward Air is our lifeline when we can't travel in *Dauntless*.
Here pilot Buddy Ferguson is carrying a mail bag for some
full-time residents in the bay.

The first addition doubled the size of Tom's workshop.

One summer this deer relaxed on our beach nearly every
afternoon for a week.

This is my favorite waterfall in our little stream. It makes a deep
pool that has at least a bit of water even in the driest times.

Tom cut and peeled small hemlocks to make the pole barn.

We never could have set the wind generator pole without the use of heavy equipment like the excavator we rented for two days.

We were lucky that Tom had prior work experience climbing utility poles.

From the platform at the top, which he can disassemble, Tom can raise or lower the metal extension pole to work on the wind generator.

We enjoy processing our own venison, at the cabin or in town.

Tom also enjoys milling lumber with his chain saw sawmill.

Stash of lumber that Tom has milled.

We've had good luck growing potatoes in barrels on the beach. This was one of our test harvests.

This bear cub was too curious, coming up the trail toward the cabin.

The cabin, with potatoes and rhubarb, before the addition was built.

Camp Borrowed Mule in session

Pops on one of his favorite rocks.

Setting foundation poles was much easier with the tractor to hoist them.

Tom made comfortable benches for our composting toilets.

The battery bank, left, allows us to store power. The
inverter, right, allows us to convert DC to AC.

Tom made our new hot water heater of copper pipe soldered
into loops that fit inside a small wood-burning stove.

The muskeg behind the cabin is a different world.

The first scrambled egg slime I found was larger than a dinner plate.

Storm surf breaking on the north reef.

Tom clearing a path to the skiff during the winter of '06.

5.

Wild Neighbors

2002

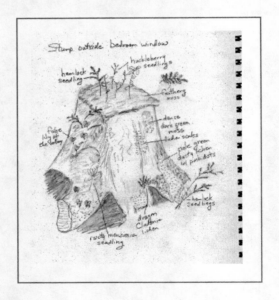

April 13 – Well, that was a unique experience. We made our first trip to the cabin this year in a small landing craft. The freight this time was a small, previously owned Kubota tractor Tom found for sale in town, a trailer full of lumber for expanding the cabin deck, and eight new aluminum propane bottles with modified safety valves required by new federal laws. The ride out was terrible. We bucked 30 knot winds all the way from Auke Bay to Point Retreat, a full hour and a half of misery. Even Tom looked a little grim when he saw green water washing over the bow and onto the little tractor he was so excited about. I was more worried about us getting drenched rather than the tractor, but the cabin, though spartan, was watertight enough, and all we suffered was a lot of lurching around and diesel smell from the big engine.

Once we rounded the point we wallowed in heavy following seas for another hour and a half to reach the bay. We turned in, taking rollers on the beam, but the skipper said there was too much crosswind to land on our beach, so we tied up at the cannery dock across the bay and waited for three hours. The wind finally dropped a little, and we motored across to our place. Tom started the tractor, and it pulled the trailer and our gear off the landing craft as smooth as ice.

So here we are. There seems to have been no wear from winter except that one solar panel on the cabin roof popped its screws and fell over; it wasn't damaged. Wind blew the metal roofing off our lumber pile, and several woodpiles partially fell over, but those are easily fixed. The stream is frozen, but Tom is melting water from the big rain catchment barrel behind his workshop to wash the salt spray off the tractor. I have reservations about having heavy equipment in our "wilderness" setting, but

I have to admit it was nice to haul the lumber and those heavy propane bottles up the beach on a trailer instead of on our backs.

May 13 – Watched two minks chasing each other across the top of our beach this morning. One was leading. When the one behind seemed reluctant to follow, it would turn around and feint; then the second would come after it. Next they both groveled low on their bellies, got up, and walked along sniffing the seaweed washed up at tideline. Then #2 turned and ran down the beach to the south, and #1 continued up toward the cabin and disappeared into the woods. What was going on? Was this a courtship display? Was the first one encouraging the second one to follow, or was it threatening #2 so it would not follow? The Department of Fish and Game Wildlife Notebook says mink breed March through April, so I'm not sure. Mink sure do have a strange loping walk, though. It's as if their front and back legs are not matched. Their long body arches up as they run, using their legs in pairs—down in front, up in back. It's a kind of teetering motion as if the pairs are conjoined and each leg can't move separately. I need to find out more about differences in the ways animals use their legs.

May 22 – Took an hour to clean seaweed off the outhaul at low tide. It's been especially hard to keep the line and pulleys clear of the slimy green hairlike weed this year. Down at mid-tide level there was a spawn of tiny periwinkles—thousands of them glued onto the brown leathery kelp fronds. Once again the sea leaves living gifts on that shifting border between land and water. I wonder how many will survive the summer. What will they eat, and what will eat them?

May 23 – Watched a yellowlegs today at the edge of the beach meadow pond. Through the binoculars I could see the beautiful gray-black patterning on its chest and the darker, more striking patterning on its wings. It teetered forward and back and flicked its tail feathers. Seemed to be grooming. Then it walked slowly through the water among the rocks, dipping its beak only an inch or two into the water, and opening and closing its beak as if it was eating something. This bird was silent, unlike the ones last year who screeched across the beach like freight trains at a crossing.

May 24 – I've decided to make a flower bed at the foot of the new path from the beach to the cabin. The established beds welcome people at the foot of the streamside path, yet this newer path is the one people are more likely to use now. So I hauled up some big rocks from the beach and filled the space with compost and soil from the area we're clearing for the cabin addition. This extends the small bed I made last year around the foxglove Donna and Dottie planted for me. Found a hunk of driftwood that looks like a totem and stood it up among the small spruce trees to form a backdrop. Will plant columbine and some lettuce tomorrow.

Tom called from Durango. I can tell he wishes he were here for this ten-day stretch—and I do, too. He keeps telling me to be careful of the bears. I'm not sure why he seems so concerned—maybe because he's not here to help manage things. I've seen only two bears this week—two dark brown ones, one scrawnier than the other, who chased each other along the beach—though night before last when I went out onto the deck after dark, I heard rustling in the grove of trees north of the cabin. The next morning I checked over there and found two bear beds – a pair of concave hollows scraped out of the soft ground.

May 25 – Had a nice slow morning. Made a fire and had a luxurious shower, then Donna paddled over in the kayak to have tea. It was warm and sunny, with no bugs, so we sat in the deck chairs down on the beach. Made sandwiches for lunch, and she left about 1 p.m.

As I came in from seeing her off, I heard Helen Peck talking w/ Phil on the CB asking if Margie was OK down at the cabin. Apparently she had heard what sounded like shots and wondered if I had a bear problem. I joined in and said all was fine here.

Took my garden tools and seeds down to the new bed on the beach. I'd made quite a bit of progress when I looked up and saw a bear on the path about 60 feet away between me and the cabin. It looked like a young one—a mound of glossy black fur over a chunky body, and at least twice my size. Its legs looked like small tree trunks. I could see its pronounced shoulder hump and the broad face with oddly small eyes. It peered at me with a cold intensity that felt at once vacant and unreachable. I stood up slowly and tried to speak firmly, from deep in my chest. "Hey, you. What are you doing here?" I said. It looked at me for a long moment, then stepped forward, twice. My stomach clenched. I had no deterrents except a pitchfork, and my heart pounded as I wondered what a young bear inexperienced with humans might do. I remembered it was important to be firm and look big, so I climbed up on a big square rock and waved my pitchfork. "Go on now. Get out of here!" I yelled. The bear just looked at me and took one more step forward.

OK, I decided. I'm outa here. But I can't run. I climbed down and started walking purposefully across

the beach. If I could make it to the path along the
stream I could go straight back to the cabin. "You can't
come down here," I said to the bear. No answer. "Go
eat someplace else," I said, as I kept walking sideways
and backward, facing the bear, which still watched me
intently. Slow down and don't stumble, I told myself.
Look strong. Now turn up the path to the cabin. But
wait. That would be circling behind the bear—a possible
sign of aggression. I turned away from the path and
waded through brush beyond the stream, keeping a big,
branched-out spruce between me and the bear. OK, now
I can turn. Cross the bridge and there are the stairs up
to the deck. The bear watched me over its shoulder till I
climbed the steps, then it turned and plodded down to
the beach. It circled to a patch of grass about five feet
from where I'd been working, looked once toward the
cabin, then began ripping out and chewing large mouthfuls of greenery.

Inside the cabin I tried to stop shaking and think
about what to do. It seemed important both to move the
bear farther down the beach and to establish the cabin
and its environs as territory where bears were unwel-
come, so I grabbed the shotgun and fired some bird shot
over the feeding bear's head. The bear jumped, and the
shot echoed across the bay, but the bear made no move
to leave or stop feeding.

I called Helen on the CB to tell her what had
happened and to be sure she knew the shot didn't signal
an emergency. "Carry a handheld VHF and call Sam if
you need help," she said, and I thanked her. But my heart
was still pounding, and I wasn't sure what to do next.
This bear was not put off by people, and if it was a
subadult just separated from its mother, it would be very

unpredictable. Even if it was just curious it could really hurt me. I didn't want to run into it on the beach again.

The grass-eating bear stayed for another half hour or so, then it headed north toward Sam and Helen's place. I was sure that if it came back our way it would come either by the beach or along the old trail between the cabins, so I went and got two sawhorses and a stack of spruce saplings and put them across the trail. A flimsy barrier like that wouldn't stop a determined bear, but it might just be troublesome enough to direct it down to the beach away from the cabin. Just for good measure I sprinkled ammonia and scattered mothballs around the barrier, hoping to make it completely obnoxious and unappealing. Then carrying the shotgun loaded with rubber pellets, I went back down to finish planting seeds. Things were great for awhile—until I looked up to see a scrawny dark brown bear walking slowly toward me along the beach. I yelled, "Hey! What are you doing here?" but it didn't slow down. I felt too vulnerable to shoot rubber pellets from there, so I turned and walked away from the garden, up the path this time, and back to the cabin. From the cabin windows, I watched the dark brown bear eat in the grassy patch for over an hour. Between bouts of ripping up grass and chewing it like some furry oversized cow, it would lie lower down on the beach with its head on its paws like a big, furry dog. I decided I would much rather wash windows in the cabin than garden anyway, and it was a relief to be able to watch the bear from the cabin without wondering where it would turn up again next.

After the bear wandered off two hours later, I went down to the beachfront garden and gathered up my tools. I decided to work in the smaller garden close to the house, and was glad of my decision when I saw a smaller bear—different from the other two, I thought—work its way across the beach to the north and past the reef to the south of us. I was able to fertilize bulbs and put in a rock border around the little garden close to the cabin, but it was nerve-wracking to be outside looking constantly over my shoulder for the next surprise. I finally came in and had dinner. Now at sunset, about 9 p.m., I can see the scrawny brown bear walking along the beach rocks from south to north. To my amazement, I can also see a deer feeding in the same grassy spot where the bears were this afternoon! As the bear moved closer, the deer turned and walked up into the woods. I suppose it was keeping its distance, but it certainly didn't seem panicked at sharing the meadow.

The scrawny brown bear looked nervous and uncertain as it came through the grass past the beach meadow pond. It turned and angled lower down the beach into the rocks, and a couple of times it hesitated and looked back over its shoulder. Was it moving away from a more dominant bear?

10:20 p.m. - Quite dark. A dark brown bear just appeared on the beach, also coming from the north. It stopped and took a long drink from our stream, then began feeding in the grass above the outhaul. I'm keeping an eye on it to see that it does not come closer to the cabin. It moved into the beach fringe and was feeding on something there for so long I began to wonder if it was bedding down for the night in the hollows under the trees. At last it moved back down onto the beach again. It just keeps on eating grass, so I suppose it's not hurting anything. I have the shotgun handy with rubber buckshot, but I won't use that unless the bear starts up the

path toward the cabin. I guess if I stay in the cabin there
should be no problem, but if Tom were here I don't
think that's what he'd do. This is definitely a different
bear from the scrawny one. It's fatter, more compact.
Walks with more confidence. But it's still small, a two-
and-a-half- or three-year-old newly on its own, I think.

Hmmm . . . I've sure spent a lot of time today
watching bears. I'm afraid now to go out and work in
the gardens. How can you shovel dirt and haul a wheelbarrow with a shotgun over your shoulder? Anyway, it's a
terrible feeling to think you're going to look up and see a
bear coming toward you at close quarters. I haven't seen
bears act like these before. They seem to have no fear of
humans or any desire to keep away from me. Sam and
Helen have left for town, and there's no one else on this
side of the bay to call if I need help. If Tom were here,
at least there'd be two of us to watch the beach and the
paths. Besides, he'd scare the bears off by being more
aggressive. But there's just one of me, and right now I
don't think I'd exude much confidence facing down a
bear.

I've been thinking, too, that my idea of planting
gardens right on the beach might not be a good one. As
I think about the houses at the head of the bay, which
have been here many more years than we have, I realize
they all have their gardens back from the beach, with a
fence or drift logs to create a barrier between the gardens
and the beach. I also realize their front decks overlook
the beach from 8 to 10 feet above ground level and they
all have railings. They're not like our deck, which is only
4 feet wide, barely at chest height above the ground,
and without any railing at all. People down there have
cleared trees and brush from in front of their cabins,

too, whereas we've left the alders and brush intact at both sides of the cabin, so we can't see the beach very far in either direction

Maybe I'll have to switch to planting boxes on the decks, or make gardens back from the driftwood line. But we face west, not south, so the only places that get sunlight for even half the day are on the beach. I wonder if we need to make some changes in our layout.

May 26 – 7:50 p.m. - The two brown bears are back. They're down on the beach in front of the wind generator pole. There must be some great-tasting grass down there. One bear is slowly walking along and eating. The other is lying on its back, rolling around and playing with its paws. If I were not worrying how I'll get past them if I want to go out in the skiff, I would really enjoy seeing them. Well, at least they're out where I can see them and not hidden behind the big rock and the drift logs.

8:07 - Here comes Walker, still munching grass. Now it lies down next to its companion.

8:09 - Lazy Boy (or Girl) just got up and started walking along eating, while Walker stays lying down.

8:12 - Walker is up and joining its buddy. Both eating steadily.

8:35 - Both bears still eating. Both are mostly dark chocolate brown with shadings of brown so light it is almost tan. Walker is now lying down and casually reaching out to munch grass within reach of its snout. Lazy Boy or Girl is lying down, too. Walker's up and moving again. Both still eating steadily. They tear up mouthfuls of grass that stick out of the sides of their mouths. They chew and they chew, then they walk along, lumbering side to side, and tear off a few more mouthfuls. When they poop they stop, hunch a little bit, and gaze straight ahead as if they're pondering some great philosophical question.

8:48 - Both bears are lying down where they'd been eating, but they're farther apart this time. In the meadow about 100 feet beyond them a lone goose is munching grass, too. Soon it starts walking around honking—crwack-crwack-crwack—but the bears are oblivious.

about 9 p.m. - One bear ate in a big half circle around the base of the wind generator pole, then it started coming up the path toward the cabin. I stood on the deck and banged an aluminum pot lid with a spoon. It looked up but seemed unwilling to turn around. I yelled and banged really hard, and it took off running into the woods. Its companion stayed sitting down on the beach, apparently unconcerned.

Maybe one thing to know is to not expect a bear, at least a young one, to change very much from the direction it is moving or seems intending to move. But the pot lid and spoon do seem to have some effect as a warning. I can begin with a slow beat, then go progressively faster and louder to increase the intensity. *Get-get-get OUT-OUT-OUT of HERE-HERE-***HERE!**

The bear that ran off has not reappeared, something I take to be a good sign. The bear on the beach is up and eating again. I think it is already bigger than the other one, and if their respective habits continue, perhaps the difference will increase.

9:20 - Well, brown bear #2 came up from the beach and onto the path to the cabin. When I stood on the deck and banged the pot lid it stopped once, but no matter how hard I banged, it kept plodding along until at last it turned aside and waddled into the woods. I can see the pot lid works as a deterrent only some of the time.

9:30 - The bears hung out on the beach for about an hour and three-quarters. Now an oystercatcher has landed and is feeding just above the water line, where the mussels are. What a treat! Those beautiful birds seldom seem to come in from the little islands out in the bay.

May 27 – Looked out the window this morning to see two bears in the front yard. It was the black one and the scrawny brown one again. They'd found the deer hide we laid back out in the woods last winter and were tugging it back and forth, fighting over it. Soon the scrawny brown one gave up tugging and started walking around and looking curious. When it started coming toward to the cabin, I went out onto the deck, yelled, and pounded on the pot lid. It jumped and ran away into the woods, but the black bear just lay there chewing on the deer hide. I was ready for that one to leave, too, so I shot some rubber buckshot toward its rump. Either I missed, or it felt nothing. It didn't even flinch. I gave up and went inside to wait it out.

9 p.m. - About noon the bears had left, so I took the skiff out for a spin. I wanted a change of scene and felt I should not stay cooped up in the cabin all day afraid of bears. Donna and Gabe came by, and they brought Polly. I gave her extra doggie treats and told her to pee all over the yard. Aren't bears supposed to be wary of dogs?

May 28 – 8 a.m. - Got up and found the scrawny brown bear rubbing its back against one of the outhaul posts, hanging its neck over the line, and pawing and chewing at the line. I could just see Tom coming home to find a wrecked outhaul to be restrung. Got the bear to leave with the Accelerated Aluminum Pot Lid Trick, but soon it came wandering back along the beach. Without stopping to eat, it came up the trail toward the cabin. Beating the pot lid finally turned it back again, but it went very slowly this time. As it walked off it kept turning and looking back. Not sure where it is now.

I'm not sure what to do. All my normal activities are being curtailed. The darn bears turn up everywhere, and I don't seem able to frighten them off. I'm afraid to burn garbage in case it might attract them. I'm afraid to put kitchen scraps in the compost for the same reason. If I work in the gardens or at the compost pile I worry about getting caught with a bear between me and the cabin. All I have is empty bravado, and I think the bears know it. I'm thinking of just going back to town today if I can charter a float plane.

What a coward! What am I going to do when we live out here full-time? I won't be able to run to town then. Tom won't be here all the time. I can't be afraid to stay here by myself. Well, right now I just want to be out of here, and I'll worry about the long term later. I'll have to haul all the garbage out and board up the place in case the bears get curious in our absence.

9 p.m. - Well, I'm packing up. Ward Air can send a float plane to pick me up at noon tomorrow.

May 29 – What a day! I packed everything this morning to go to town, then twenty minutes before the plane was due, one of the two dark brown bears came waltzing down the beach. It lay down next to the outhaul, laid its head down onto its paws, and went to sleep—right where I had to walk out to catch the plane. I stacked my gear on the front deck and boarded up the windows anyway, but I left the front door unlocked in case I needed to go back in. As the plane approached, the pilot must have spotted the bear because he veered over the beach and buzzed right over the bear's head. The bear cocked

its head and looked up, but it didn't budge. The plane
swung around and buzzed low a second time, and the
bear finally seemed to get the message. It scrambled to
its feet and loped into the woods. I shut and locked the
front door, grabbed my gear off the deck, and started
down the path to the beach—but the plane had turned
and was flying back toward town! I ran back to the cabin,
unlocked the door, and plugged in the phone to call
Ward Air. "Charlene, this is Marge. My charter flew over
the beach, but then it turned around and headed back
toward town. Where's he going?" It took all the energy I
had not to yell. "Hang on for a minute," the dispatcher
said. There were a few minutes of silence, then she came
back. "The pilot thought you wouldn't come out when
there was a bear on the beach," she said.

"I'll come out! I'll come out!" Was that me yelling?
"Tell him to come back. Get me out of here!"

"OK, he's on his way."

There was no point in waiting inside the cabin.
With all the front windows boarded up I couldn't see
the beach. So I went out onto the deck again, locked the
door, and waited on that flimsy four feet of planks for
the plane to come back. I was beyond being surprised
when, as I heard the drone of the plane approaching,
here came the bear, walking across the beach toward the
outhaul again. The pilot buzzed the beach again, nearly
brushing the bear's head for all I could see, and this time
the bear headed for the woods on a dead run. I grabbed
my duffle bag, day pack, shotgun, and a week's worth of
garbage, and ran for my life across 200 feet of low tide
beach to the plane. I don't think I stopped shaking the
whole way to town. Now that I think about it, I feel silly
again, but what could I have done differently?

June 8 – Flew out with Tom on Ward Air. The whole neighborhood is here. There are people in all six cabins. It's better here with two of us, and Tom is armed with cracker shells and nonlethal rounds that deliver a punch but don't seriously harm a bear. People have been seeing bears on the beaches everywhere. The dark brown bear that doesn't run came by in the afternoon and was eating grass right by the beach garden again. Tom went down and yelled at it, but it ignored him. He shot it in the rear end with one of the nonlethals, and you could see it jump. It ran off a little way, then ambled slowly away. When it came along the beach later on, it stayed way down by the water.

June 9 – This morning the dark brown bear crossed our beach again, and we were very pleased it stayed down near the water. Later, about 4:30, we saw the bear high on the beach far to the north. It stayed in the grass there, eating and napping, but never approached the cabin. I hope we've established some good parameters, at least with one bear. There's been no sign of the other three.

July 21 – I spotted a heron in the big hemlock above the woodshed this morning and watched it groom itself. It lifted one, then the other long, gangly leg and used its toes and toenails to smooth its coat. It pulled and smoothed feathers with its beak, and rubbed its head with its wings. Then it lifted off, its big wings thrashing the branches, and glided away toward the beach. Why does a big water bird perch in a tree where its big wings seem to tangle in a thicket of branches?

August 31 – Made potato soup with fresh spuds from our beach garden barrels. The plants have not died down yet, but we dug a few early reds and whites. Looks as if we'll have a good crop again this year.

September 13 – Took the skiff over to the two salmon streams to look for bears today, but found birds instead. Bald eagles were clustered along both streams—maybe ten immatures and at least five adults. Even the immatures were beautiful in their splotchy plumage—a wide variety of variegated white and brown. One had its fully white head feathers but still had a splotchy body and no white tail. Was it a four-year-old close to maturity? We watched two immatures fight over a salmon carcass. After a flurry of pecking and flapping, one darted and jabbed at the other enough to drive it off, then it half spread its wings over the prize—"mantling," as my book on raptors says. Farther upstream five more eagles and a cluster of ravens leaped and fluttered, messing with something in the grass above the stream bank. Herring and Bonaparte gulls pattered or stood along shore. As we rowed over the sandbar, we could see that the bottom of the water was littered with salmon carcasses lying only a few inches apart. When do the crabs come for them, I wondered? And still there were crowds of salmon struggling upstream and milling around at the mouth. Dark fins broke the water everywhere, and every few moments, when some stimulus created panic or maybe just some wild impulse cut loose, an entire group of fish would flush, veering off in a clap and flash of swirling water.

After awhile the bears arrived, and we watched them from a good distance offshore in the skiff. A sow and two half-grown cubs splashed after fish in the nearest stream, the sow finally dragging a salmon to shore, followed by the cubs. While the bears were tearing at the fish, a somewhat larger bear approached along the beach from the south. The adult bears eyed each other but stayed quite a distance apart, then finally the sow and cubs turned and walked up into the woods. Were they satiated, or keeping a safe distance from their neighbor? I wasn't sure, but apparently there's enough food these days so that no one gets overly excited about having company nearby.

September 15 – Worked hard clearing some more stumps around the cabin this weekend. Tom installed a short chainlink fence with a gate to replace my sawhorse-and-pole bear barrier across the trail. If it works we'll see bears only on the beach, or well away from the cabin.

October 20 – Well, this time it was Tom who had the bear adventure. He'd been at the cabin alone hunting and putting in wood, and then it was time to leave. He'd closed up the cabin to walk up the bay about half a mile, where he would meet a float plane scheduled to take him and one of our neighbors back to Juneau. Tom said he had seen no bears, tracks, or bear sign the whole week, and though we always carry the shotgun when we travel to and from the cabin, he had thought of zipping it into its canvas case so it would be ready to put on the plane. For some reason he didn't.

Tom said he'd walked along the brushy trail from the cabin about 600 feet to where it opens into Sam's Cove when suddenly, about 20 feet away at the top of the beach meadow, he saw a large sow with two cubs digging up lupine roots. He thought the sow could not see him very well because he was in front of a small spruce tree and was wearing his green raincoat, but she knew he was there. As soon as he saw her he yelled out loud, "Hup, Bear!" She crashed forward into the brush that was between them, and the cubs began to run—one of them back toward her and one directly toward Tom.

Tom immediately backed up, shouting so the sow would know where he was and that he wasn't another bear, and hoping that would also convince the cub to back away. The sow huffed even more and began ripping up the brush around her with her claws. Tom kept yelling, "Hup, Bear! Hup, Bear!" and backing away as fast as he could. Finally the cub turned around, the sow corralled both cubs, and the three bears ran off into the woods. Tom said the whole encounter took place in about ten seconds.

So often it seems that we come upon bears just after a long spell of not seeing any sign of them at all. I guess that tells me we can't assume they're not around just because we don't see them. We need to remember they wander this country pretty much at will, and there's no time of year, not even winter, when you can be dead sure you won't run into one.

December 20 – Good week hunting and enjoying the cabin. Temperature last night dropped to 28 degrees, but we are snug and warm.

December 21 – Winter Solstice at 8:15 p.m. We stood on the frozen beach in the blustering wind and lit a fire to celebrate. Now the light turns around, and we get to start a new year.

6.

Consolidating

2003

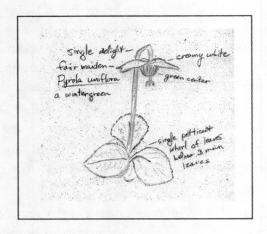

January 15 – I'm house-sitting at the head of the bay while Phil and Donna travel down South for two weeks. The house has a diesel generator for lights, and oil heat supplemented by wood, but I will be cut off from town, especially if the weather is bad, so I've tried to prepare for any contingencies. It was 18 degrees when I left town yesterday morning, so cold will be the main thing to deal with, especially since I want to spend some time outside hiking and exploring. Brought my heavy fleece hunting coat, two fleece hats, three pairs of wool gloves, insulated rubber gloves, ice creepers, fleece pants, warm pajamas, turtlenecks, and extra long johns. I also packed six cardboard boxes of food, my laptop computer, binoculars, camera, cell phone, wallet, and two briefcases of materials for writing projects. It's interesting to see what I do not want to live without! Tom flew out, too, to help me get settled in, but tomorrow he has to leave to go back to work.

This morning we took our skiff down the bay to check on our cabin. It's a cold ride at this time of year. Still, this cold doesn't feel as chilling as the wind and rain we had back in December. Our big project for today was to take the blades off the wind generator for the winter. Tom climbed 60 feet up the pole to his work platform, removed three boards so he could climb onto it, then reassembled it for a workspace. He lowered the generator on its collapsible metal pipe, then removed the three blades. I stayed at the bottom of the pole manning the pulley line, sending up a bucket with the tools he needed, and pulling down the blades and tools when he was finished. All went smoothly despite a bitter wind, and the generator won't be beating itself to death in winter gales when we're not there to use it.

On the beach in front of the cabin the new rhubarb root I'd planted near our barrel garden site had been washed out by an extremely high tide. Who'd have thought the tide would come up to the oldest drift logs? I found a hollow partway up the rock ledge facing the beach and expanded it with a wall of stacked rocks, then filled it with soil from a patch of garden that was not yet completely frozen. It's quite appropriate, I think, that a piece of this root, which Tom's dad brought us from Michigan, is being planted right next to Pops's favorite "settin' spot." I suppose if it doesn't do well we'll have to have Pops come out to encourage it with a little smoke from his pipe.

Looking at the level of this highest tide, I also decided to disassemble the rock gardens I'd started along the front edge of the old drift logs. I will let the ocean have its way with the front yard for now (and be thankful we moved our garden barrels back from the beach for the winter).

We pulled the skiff out of the water and onto the trailer, then Tom used the tractor to put it behind the generator shed for the winter. We walked back to the head of the bay along the low-tide rocks. It was good to be dressed in sturdy winter gear. The wind blew against us for the whole mile and a half.

March 30 – The landing craft arrived today with materials for the cabin addition. We'd planned for an early March delivery so the ground would still be frozen, but the landing craft was diverted for some more crucial errand, so the date was delayed. Now, with temperatures in the 40s, the beach is pretty well thawed, and the fork-lift had to churn through mud to move the pallets across the beach and up to the new materials storage site. Our tractor trail also proved to be too narrow, so I had to tear apart one side of the rock garden to get it out of the way of the big tires. We managed to get all eight pallets moved into place, though, and the landing craft left without incident—a great relief.

There's lots of wildlife around even though there's not much other sign of spring. I'm beginning to know the cast of players by heart. Two Canada geese flew from the beach meadow when we arrived. Two herons came to feed in the beach meadow pond. Ravens and eagles are about. Out on the water: a striking gray loon with white on its breast and the front of its neck, several harlequin ducks, six buffleheads, four goldeneyes, a couple of mergansers. Varied thrush and winter wren are singing in the woods. A red-breasted sapsucker is tapping in the snag on the north end of the lot, and pine siskins and chickadees are cheeping high in the trees. There are deer tracks and droppings on trails and in the gardens, and Tom saw a mink before I got up this morning.

The new rhubarb root is sprouting in its second home, and the creeping Charlie that Donna gave me last summer is up beneath the big hemlock out front. No grass is sprouting in the meadow yet, though. Snow still lies in drifts on the south side of cabin, and the kitchen garden in what we call the "north wind freeze corridor" is still frozen solid. Small patches of the stream are beginning to thaw, but most of it is still thickly coated with ice and snow. We were surprised at dusk to see a bat flying across the front of the cabin.

June 28 – Haven't written much the last three months. I came back to the cabin today on the mail plane and am looking forward to a week here till Tom comes out after his shift ends on Thursday. Progress on the addition has been slow so far this summer. All four exterior walls and the tongue-and-groove ceiling boards (Layer 1 of the roof) are up, but that's as far as we got. Tom was quite concerned when I told him on the phone that the two small tarps we'd tied on under the big main tarp covering the building had blown loose in the wind. He said the ceiling boards will be wrecked if they get wet. So I spent more than two hours trying to drag the lower tarps back into place, working off both ladders and crawling around on the roof with the main tarp flapping over my head where I'd loosened its tie-downs. It was nerve-wracking trying to crawl around up there, and I worried that I was going to slide off. I don't think there was any real danger, but a couple of times I had to grab the peak of the roof or jab the claw of the hammer into the ridge between two boards so I could sit still and catch my breath for a minute. It was a tremendous relief when Dottie and Collie stopped by on a hike up the beach from their cabin on the point. Collie helped me with the last, most difficult, fastenings.

As it turned out, the worst part was getting down after Dottie and Collie had left. The ladder on the south side didn't seem stable when I eased down the roof and put my foot on it, so I crawled across the roof and used the ladder on the north side instead. Made it okay, but I hope I don't have to do this again. I was so glad to have proof the job was worth the effort that I nearly cheered when it started raining hard and blowing again about 5 p.m.

June 29 – Great pleasure and excitement this morning. I spent two hours marking out estimated locations for my desk, bookcases, and other furniture in the addition so Tom will know where to put the wood stove. I spent the afternoon scraping stain off the front exterior of the main cabin. It's hard, messy work, but it looks as if we'll have to scrape all the walls down to get at the mildew growing under the stain's hard UV-protective layer. What a project! This time I used both the heat gun and supposedly nontoxic citrus stripper to loosen the stain, then used a putty knife to scrape it off in inch-wide strips. The deck is littered with grocery bags full of paper towels gummed up with scraped-off stain in globs and long, curly spirals, and both my arms ache. Ugh!

Larry and Angela have brought me Dungeness crabs twice this week. They've been working long hours on building their own dome-shaped house overlooking the sandy beach, but still they find time to run their pots and be neighborly. Lucky me!

July 14 – Well, I've had twenty full days at the cabin this trip. Tom arrived two days ago, and we got lots done on the addition. We also had wonderful help over Fourth of July from Lucy and John and two of their Coast Guard friends and their teenage son. When they all offered to come out and help, Tom teased that we would "work 'em like borrowed mules," so we ended up calling their three days here "Camp Borrowed Mule." They did all work very hard, and thanks to their help we made a major step forward: the roof is on and the interior of the building is protected from the rain. Seems we should be able to relax and go at a slower pace now.

July 25 – Today was the third of ten days on my own at the cabin, but it was not fun. I woke up with pain in my left hand and at breakfast could hardly open it or use it to lift anything. I guess I overdid scraping on the exterior walls yesterday, so I decided to do something using different muscles. The weather was clear and sunny, with a forecast of more of the same, so I spent the day scrubbing down the exterior walls of the addition according to the preparation instructions for a new kind of stain we'll be applying there.

It's so cumbersome to do something like this without the running water and household electricity we take for granted in town. Tom set everything up before he left, but I still got flustered trying to keep all the equipment going and get everything done within the proper time specifications. First you have to mix the proper proportions of water, bleach, and trisodium phosphate, and spray them onto the walls with a pump-up garden sprayer. Then you scrub the wet walls with a brush on the end of a broom handle to loosen oils on the milled wood that would reject stain. After twenty minutes you wash the solution off with a pressure washer and scrub the walls again with the brush. Because we have no running water, the pressure washer is fed by a hose from a small portable pump Tom put down on the bottom of the rainwater barrel. You have to run the diesel generator to power both the pump and the pressure washer, and keep their long extension cords from tangling. I probably looked like a one-woman circus running from one cabin wall to another, hauling my ladders and leveling them on uneven ground with chunks of 2-by-4s, then dragging along the throbbing black pressure washer with wheels that jerked to a stop every time they hit a loose rock, and a hose and power cord that tangled on every stick and tree root in sight. When I tried to wash under the eaves, the water and bleach solution poured down till I was soaked all over no matter how hard I tried to avoid the drips, and of course every sprayer nozzle got clogged at least three times.

I was really grateful to finish without any mechanical problems, but then I found that something—maybe oils that washed down or the scrubbing solution—had made big dark patches on all the windows, which it had not occurred to me to cover. I scrubbed each blotch with mineral spirits and Windex, and they seemed to clear up; but, no, when the glass dried off the streaks, patches, and smears were still there. For an hour or two I panicked, thinking the solution had etched the glass and ruined all the windows. Wouldn't that be great to announce to Tom! It would be more than a disaster. Finally, after much trial and error, I found I could scrape off most of the smears with a razor blade, wash the remains off with brush cleaner, then restore the clear glass with Windex. It took me an hour to clean one window, so I have five to go, plus the sliding glass doors, which I think are not as badly smeared as the windows. I nearly called Dottie and Collie and told them I was too tired to come to dinner, but I'm glad I didn't. Now that I'm home after a very nice evening with them, I feel a lot better. Maybe tomorrow I can start staining the ceiling in the addition. Right now I'm just looking forward to the day when all the building is done and we can get back to enjoying our time out here.

August 8 – This morning I watched a woodpecker—a downy or a hairy, I think, because it was black and white with a red patch on the back of its head. It was feeding in a spruce tree near the workshop. The bird was only 5 or 6 feet above my eye level, so I could see it clearly. It hopped along two different horizontal branches, spiraling completely around each branch, pecking errati- cally (maybe only when it sensed something to eat?). Both branches were dead ones without needles. Then it flew to another spruce tree where I could no longer see it as well. I wonder what it's getting to eat.

August 13 – Worked with help from Donna for three days and nearly finished putting three coats of stain on all the exterior walls of the addition and the front wall and roof overhang of the main cabin. We pushed really hard to finish before the weather turned bad again, and Tom and Lucy came out from town and helped us wrap up the job yesterday. The addition looks beautiful. The walls are a tawny butterscotch with the grain and knots in the wood showing through. I can't wait till it's set up as a little haven where Tom and I can relax and I can write.

August 15 – Good family times this week, as Tom's dad and Lucy are back for a visit. They both seem impressed with our work on the addition, and Pops approved the new location for the rhubarb. We all walked to the sandy beach yesterday and watched crowds of spawning pink salmon fight their way up the second creek. It was good to see the amazing annual spectacle again and to reflect on the continuing cycles between the sea and the land.

Later, at about 4 p.m., I looked out the window and saw Tom and his dad moving the outhouse—this less than two hours before we had five guests due to arrive for dinner. I only hoped they'd be done before the company arrived, and thank goodness they were. I'm looking forward to the new arrangement. We'll use the same little building to house the outdoor "facilities," but we plan to switch from outhouse mode to a composting system. It seems so much better to try to return our waste to usable condition as soon as possible, and I have never liked the idea of just collecting it in a big barrel that starts to smell no matter how much you try to treat it. This time we're going to use 5-gallon buckets and peat moss—the same system we put in to replace the Sun-Mar composting toilet in the main cabin last year. (I decided I didn't like the waste sitting inside the cabin for so long, even if it was enclosed in a revolving drum and supposedly breaking down.) Joe Jenkins describes the bucket system in *The Humanure Handbook*, and it seems to make a lot of sense. It's really just an improvement on the old honey bucket, but when you use generous scoopfuls of peat moss there is no smell, and since you empty the bucket every few days, none of the material stays indoors long enough to attract flies or develop odors. Joe has gathered lots of scientific research to show that once the material is outdoors in the holding pile, it breaks down into usable soil within a few years. I think the composting will take longer in our cool climate, but we have room to keep several piles if we need them. They'll be well away from the kitchen compost piles and the working areas of our lot, and we have lots of seaweed, alder leaves, and weeds to keep feeding them. If the book is correct, the resulting soil should be hygienically safe, though we'll keep it clear of the vegetable gardens and the stream just in case.

August 18 – Worked hard with Tom, Lucy, and Pops yesterday hauling brush and stumps to burn in a big fire on the beach. With some of the worst brush piles cleaned up, the area around the cabin looks like an idyllic natural landscape. The ferns flare up in the front yard like giant bouquets, and the mossy logs look like miniature gardens with all their seedlings and tiny green plants. After sweating and fighting off bugs while we hauled brush, it was absolute heaven to build a fire in the water heater and each take a nice hot shower. What is it about hot water running over our bodies that's so luxurious? I would haul a hundred cords of wood to keep that luxury going. (Well, for this year maybe four or five cords will do.)

September 12 – I finally got outside and moved the steppingstones from the old outhouse route to make a path to the new one. I'm not sure why these little paths please me so much, but they do. I know they detract from the sense of true "wilderness" I thought I wanted, but I love the way they curve from place to place; and I have such pleasant memories of taking the skiff to the cove across the bay to pick up flat rocks. Even scratching up the soil and planting the rocks so they're firm and stable is really rewarding. Seems as if it might all be a combination of the impulse toward nest-building and a desire for pretty surroundings. At any rate, the paths are a special pleasure—not the least of which is having a firm footing over uneven ground, and steps across the mud in wet weather.

September 20 – The hot-water heater has sprung a leak. We're managing to keep it going, but the firebox is getting soggier and soggier, and Tom doesn't think he can get the unit apart for repairs without wrecking it. We're not sure what we'll do. The company that makes this unit has apparently gone out of business, and we haven't been able to find another wood-fired heater that you can operate safely indoors.

November 30 – The end of our Thanksgiving week at the cabin. This afternoon we're in the midst of a fierce snowstorm. The wind is beating against the front of the cabin, and snow is swirling across the beach meadow and the front yard. The waves crashing onto the beach look at least 3 feet high, the biggest I've ever seen in our little cove. On the beach they tumble forward and plunge their foamy white caps down onto the rocks. Against the ledge they slam in head first, sending up plumes of spray. I can't even see out to the reefs to see what's happening there. To add to the wildness the wind generator is howling as if to tear itself apart. I guess this is when you appreciate all those extra tie-downs and nails and screws you put into a well-built cabin.

By tomorrow, when we're scheduled to fly back to town, we'll have been here for seven wonderful days. We had good hunting—Tom got two nice bucks on a ridge behind the cabin, though I never saw a deer in time to shoot. On two mornings in a row we had fresh snow. I followed deer tracks along the muskeg and into the woods, but I never caught up with the track-makers— even when I came back in the afternoon and found their tracks on top of mine! But I did find two fresh beds—ovals of green under low-hanging trees, where a deer had lain and melted the snow so the moss showed through. On Thanksgiving morning, when we were hunting under the big trees near the avalanche chute, a marten ran up to within 20 feet of me. There it was, just loping along, a brown, cat-sized animal with perky ears and a fluffy tail. When it saw me it screeched to a stop, hesitated, ran sideways a bit, peered intently at me, then took off running. Tom saw it, too, though he was quite far ahead of me by then.

As we walked home by way of the beach we saw a group of five otters diving and feeding in the water. One came up with a dark, roundish lump that we think was probably a crab. The others had silvery fishes that looked at least 5 or 6 inches long.

We had a few water problems when we arrived last Tuesday, a result of the unexpected cold snap. The big water-catchment barrel had frozen and tipped over, dumping the gravel-filled strainer bucket on top of it onto the ground. The hose that runs from there to the storage barrels below the cabin had also frozen. Fortunately, we'd disconnected and emptied the Omni whole-house filter in that line, so we won't have the trouble and expense of replacing that as we did last year; but we hadn't emptied and blown out the copper lines to the bathroom and kitchen, so the shower handle and controls froze and broke, and the special faucet for drinking water in the kitchen cracked. Tom was able to redirect the pipes for now. He cut off the bathroom run so we could get water to the kitchen from the storage barrels beneath the cabin, which didn't freeze. Then I figured out that we could bypass the cracked faucet and pump filtered water into a holding jug for drinking, so we made out just fine. We put some thought into what our other alternatives might be in freezing weather and decided we could melt snow or boil stream water for drinking, or pump water by the bottleful through the small backpacking filter system we keep in the kitchen. We may have to do that at Christmastime if the storage barrels under the house run out or freeze.

December 25 – Christmas Day – Half an inch of very wet snow fell during the night, but we're snug and warm in the cabin. We'd planned to spend Christmas with Donna and Phil and their kids, but Gabe and Phil have some kind of bug so we'll hold off for this week. I set up a small spruce bough on the bookcase in the living room and decorated it with silver garlands and four of our favorite red ornaments. Tom's rigged up temporary running water again, and the turkey roll is in the oven. With Christmas music on my portable CD player, and the wood stove humming away, it feels like the perfect quiet Christmas in our cozy nest.

Had a great wildlife show earlier today. From the big dining-room window I watched mergansers doing their courtship displays. There were three males and two females in a fairly tight group, paddling around just off the low-tide shoreline. As they swam along, the males kept lifting their bills up, tipping their heads back, then quickly dipping their bodies down into the water and up again. They held their bills open and seemed to take sips from the water as they dipped down and up. One of the females was very active. At least three times I saw her glide toward a male, then mirror what he did: sipping from the surface of the water, opening her bill wide, tipping her head back, pointing her bill to the sky, then dipping her body down and back up. What seemed odd was that whenever a male approached her, the female would dart toward him with her bill wide open as if threatening to bite, and the offending male would lunge away with a splash. Every so often all three males and the female would rear up in the water and flap their wings. Meanwhile, all the second female did was swim around in circles and spirals, though several times the first female swam aggressively between her and a male. What a show—probably the merganser equivalent of a singles bar.

December 27 – Time to pack up and close the cabin for the season. We'll fly back to town for Tom's next shift later this afternoon. Tom unhooked the water again, and we've put antifreeze in all the drains. The fridge is cleared out with the door propped open, and the wood stove is nearly cold. With the plywood "bear boards" covering all but the big dining-room window (the last one to be covered), the place feels abandoned and gloomy. The addition looks a little less grim. We don't feel a need to board up its windows, and I'm glad we decided not to install any plumbing there. Still, it's hard to leave. Sometimes it seems we'll never get to that day when we'll live here full-time, without having to pack up and leave every week or two. But I guess April will come soon enough.

7.

What It's For

2005

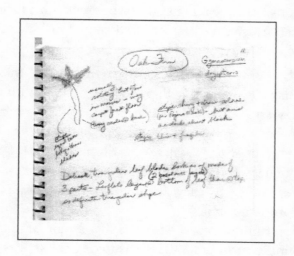

April 7 – First day of a new season, and I'm reminded why we want so much to make our life out here. Twenty-some goldeneyes bob in the cove in front of the cabin. They cluster in a tight flock, intricate black and white plumage shape-shifting as the birds jockey for position. North of them, three buffleheads and six mergansers dive for fish then pop up, one by one, like champagne corks. Earlier today six sea lions splashed by, and an otter curled through the water and disappeared behind the reef.

Onshore, two yellowlegs patter along the water's edge, and all the other regulars are back. Two Canada geese fly over the meadow honking. The ravens are raucous in the big trees on the point, and chickadees and siskins are squeaking high in the trees. This morning Tom heard this year's first varied thrush. Look what we'd be missing if we'd stayed back in town.

April 8 – Two herons came to the beach meadow pond this morning. They flapped along shore with those long, lazy strokes, then set down like shadows near the outflow. Both crouched low and padded slowly through the grass. Step. Stop. Step. Wait. Step again. One stops and crouches. The other minces along the water's edge, then steps in. Are they feeding cooperatively, or just being companionable?

I don't know, but they move like a pair of dancers. Each bundle of gray feathers has two sticklike legs, each shadow has a long neck and white breast feathers that flutter in the breeze. The still one cocks its head sideways, one eye peering into the pond. Then it stiffens, and its head swivels upright. The long neck stretches forward, inches down, down, down. Then, *zap!* Head and neck stab the water. The beak lifts, dripping. A small fish is clamped in the beak's hammer tongs, and they mouth it once, twice, and again. The heron flicks its head and seems to swallow, then stands motionless, staring straight ahead. Now the neck curves forward, and the beak combs once, twice through the fluffy breast plumes. The killing tool is for grooming now, all part of a day and a life. Knees dip and the bird launches, a gray flag unfurling into the wind.

April 17 – Late last night Tom and I heard a telltale smacking, and we rushed down to the beach. At the mouth of the bay two humpbacks were leaping out of the water and crashing down. Others were diving and surfacing, and one lay on its side, smacking the surface with its long, armlike flipper. This time we could hear their cattlelike braying and groaning. A mink came down to the beach, spotted us, and hastily beat it back up into the woods. On the walk back we could see that a bear had dropped fresh sign along the tractor trail, and the deer have nibbled every new skunk cabbage sprout down to the nub.

I think this will be a big spruce pollen year. The yellow dust is coating everything—decks, roofs, bare ground, and the surface of the water. The filter for the water catchment barrel was clogged with goop that looked like sticky yellow pudding, and the barrel lid had an eighth-inch layer glommed onto its underside.

I think it will be a big crossbill year, too. Flocks of twenty or thirty at a time have come through the yard every day. They land like small whirlwinds in the trees, then plummet to the ground like hailstones. I like the contrast between the red males and the olive-green females, and this year I've twice seen brown-streaked birds that aren't errant siskins, as I'd first thought. *The*

Sibley Guide to Birds says they are juvenile crossbills, less than a year old. It seems odd that some birds patter along and peck at scattered spruce cones on the ground, while others pick up individual cones, carry them to branches a few yards up, and perch there, plucking seeds with the rhythm of small sewing machines. I wonder if getting off the ground is a precaution against predation. Perhaps it's not enough to confuse predators with the chaos of movement the flock creates as it skitters around. Alternate measures may be important, and I wonder if individual birds feed in all these different ways, or if some habitually use one way more than the others. After a few minutes, the birds fly off, and I'm reminded how easily I could miss scenes like this if I didn't go about my chores with one eye cocked toward the windows.

April 19 – This morning five harlequins are hanging around the exposed reef. What a contrast—the females are drab brown, while the males sport blue-gray plumage with a patchwork of white spots, white stripes, and rust-brown flanks. All three males swim over to a female perched on a rock. They peer up at her, lift their heads, stretch their necks, and flutter their tails. She watches their display, opens her beak in response, then plunges into the water. The males paddle madly after her as she circles, climbs back onto the reef, and languidly stretches, arching her neck and delicately fluttering her wings.

Later, all five birds are on the water. They're all milling around, diving to feed and then popping up again, or swimming along with just their beaks underwater. Even from the cabin I can hear their little squeaking sounds. They sound like bathtub toys or the rubber mice my kids buy for their cat. Suddenly the three males veer off after one of the females—is it Miss Popularity again? One male stands up in the water and madly flaps his wings. The female does the same, then all four birds stretch their necks and bob their heads up and down. The other female swims along behind—alone. I hope she's designated wallflower for only a day.

May 24 – We're making great progress on the cabin addition. Tom installed the vanity and wash basin, plumbed the basin drain to the gray-water line, hung the bathroom door, and installed a bench, vent pipe, and seat for our third composting toilet unit. A "cabin" with three bathrooms! Things are getting pretty up-town. We finished off the old outhouse site by piling a heap of rocks over it and planting a garden.

In the main cabin Tom reinstalled the wood-fired hot water system, which he'd disassembled for the winter. The system he put in last year works well, and it takes up only a little more space in the living room than the old commercially-made heater did. To make the new system, Tom soldered 18 feet of 3/4-inch copper pipe and fittings into a series of loops that fit around the inside of the firebox of a small wood-fired Yukon stove. The house plumbing system feeds cold water into the tubes, which heat up when we make a fire in the stove. As the water heats up, it moves by thermal siphon action into an adjacent 20-gallon electric water heater that's not hooked up to work electrically. When we light a fire in the evening and kept it going for half an hour or so, we heat all the water in the tank to about 120 degrees F., and it stays hot for about 24 hours. There's a safety valve on the tank, of course, but we just watch the attached thermometer so we don't get the temperature so high the tank would need to blow off steam. It's great to have a reliable hot water system again.

Four sets of neighbors at our end of the bay arrived this week, so we attended the usual round of dinners and "beer:30" cocktail hours. I spent so much time cleaning, managing compost piles, cooking meals, and playing hostess, there was no time to write.

June 8 – Tom's brother Rob and his wife Cyndie's visit to the cabin was a resounding success. They were bowled over by Southeast's water and mountains just as I'd hoped they'd be, since it's such a contrast to Michigan. Cyndie and I loved cooking together and laughing at the sibling banter between Rob and Tom. They both helped us haul a new propane refrigerator up the beach and into the main cabin. The old bear-thrashed fridge has been consigned to beer and pop duty in Tom's workshop. It's so satisfying to see people we love enjoying the guest space in the addition, and it's gratifying to show them the kind of life we're building out here.

This is Cyndie's first trip to Alaska, Rob's third. When Rob was here in '96, it rained hard every day, so he'd warned Cyndie to pack two sets of rain gear, and told her she should expect rain most of the time. Instead, it's been sunny with light winds the whole week. The trip from town was so idyllic I half thought we'd stumbled into one of those panoramic photos the visitor industry uses to lure people up here: snow-peaked mountains pierced clear blue skies, the forests were velvet green along the shore, and the water was a carpet of glittering blue-green. The only things missing were bikinis and a trayful of gin and tonics in the cockpit. We saw humpback whales feeding and diving at four different points along the way, and to Cyndie's delight a pod of five Dall porpoise rode our bow wave near Point Retreat and stayed with us for nearly half a mile.

Yesterday, satiated with two days of chores and leisurely time-outs for meals and the books we all brought, we packed a lunch and fired up *Dauntless* to take Rob and Cyndie fishing. It was another spectacularly beautiful day, with bright sun and just a slight breeze—not the kind of weather we take for granted in Southeast. We passed sea lions feeding off the south entrance to the bay, and saw several humpbacks spouting and diving just a couple of miles to starboard. Rob must have photographed twenty different eagles perched in trees along the shore of the island, and he practically fell out of the cockpit trying to get close-ups of a couple that flew directly overhead and across the water.

Fishing was slow. We trolled a quarter mile behind another pleasure boat, hoping those folks knew more about fishing hot spots than we did, but our lines just bobbled along behind the boat. I don't think anyone really cared. With warm sun, spectacular scenery, and plenty of food and good company, none of us cared a whole lot if we caught any fish.

We'd all settled into a contented torpor when Tom, who was driving the boat, said, "Look. I think there are some killer whales up ahead." We finally made out what he was seeing: what looked like skinny black sticks poking up above the water some distance in front of the boat ahead. Sure enough, the sticks were moving. Soon we saw the flash of dark backs and dorsal fins. I was excited because we don't see killer whales as often as humpbacks in our area, and we hadn't seen any yet near the cabin this summer.

"Look," Tom said. "They're heading straight toward that boat . . . now they're moving past it on both sides." How odd, I thought. Wouldn't you think they'd swim away from a large vessel and the noise of its engine? On they came, and it began to dawn on us that the whales were not only holding a steady course. They were headed right toward us. Maybe we'd get to see them really close up. "Wow! There are six . . . no, eight of them," I shouted. We saw plumes of spray shoot out of the water, then behind each one came the flash of a black back and the curve of a sharklike fin. Closer and closer they came, a phalanx of synchronized swimmers. Eight white plumes. Eight black backs. Eight dorsal fins. But one fin was much taller and straighter than the others. Triumphant banner of a large male, it must have reached 6 feet into the air.

The whales dove, and for a moment there was nothing. Rob, Cyndie, and I ran back to the cockpit. We dashed from side to side, peering ahead of the boat. Where would the whales surface next? I scrambled up the ladder to the flying bridge. No, it's better to see them from the cockpit. I hurried down to see them at eye level. Look, there they are, right next to the boat!

"See that? Look! Look!" We were yelling, pointing, leaning over each other as whales surfaced at what seemed barely arm's length away on both sides of us. Whoosh! Curve. Dip. We could see gray saddle patches and white foreflanks. Then nothing again.

I ran into the cabin to check with Tom. "Did you see that? They were right next to the boat!" His grin looked a little forced, and I realized he was standing very straight with both hands gripping the wheel. "Ah," I said. "They were pretty close, eh?" "Yeh," he said. "I slowed down, but I felt like I was driving the wrong way on the freeway."

Behind the boat, the whales surfaced several more times before they faded out of sight. Sticks again, they swam tight along the shore, diving, blowing, surfacing in perfect rhythm. Rob, Cyndie, and I crowded into the cabin with Tom, breathless and dazed. Rob is not a religious or philosophical man, but, "That was incredible," he said. "Everyone in the world should get to experience something like that. What a feeling to be so close to something so massive and impressive." I think I was as overwhelmed as he was, but I thought, too: Tom and I live here. What a place we've chosen to be in. What a privilege to be here.

June 13 – Saw an adult goshawk on the south lot this afternoon. I was alerted by the persistent squawking of two Steller's jays and three strident "mews" of a woodpecker. When I went to investigate I saw the Stellers were flying back and forth around a large tan bird perched in a scrawny hemlock. I ran back to the cabin and got Tom out of his workshop, and we both went for a better look. It was a male goshawk all right. It was bigger than a raven, and I could see a dark mask around the eyes and a white streak above the forehead. "Look," Tom said. "Its eyes are red." When it turned its head in profile we saw several downy feathers stuck to its beak. It must have just eaten a young bird. The Stellers finally flew off, but the goshawk stayed on its branch, staring down at us. It looked fierce and unflappable. Obviously the world was centered 20 feet above our heads, but I had no inclination to venture there.

July 27 – Tom wants to build a hydroplant in our little stream. He thinks we could get enough power when it's rainy in the fall to supplement what we get from the wind generator and the solar panels. But it would mean running a 2-inch white plastic pipe 500 feet down the stream from back in the muskeg. He's asked Sam and

Andy for permission to run pipe back there, and to install a catchment barrel in a large pool where the water gathers before it flows downgrade into our stream.

I'm sick at the thought of an ugly plastic pipe running down our idyllic little stream. How could a pipe bend to fit all the little curves? Could it run under the root wads and the little fern-covered mounds the stream tunnels through? No, it would have to lie up on the banks to get around them, a glaring plastic eyesore poking out from each pretty riffle and clump of beautiful green moss.

How can I say, "Yeh, sure. Go ahead"? Tom loves challenges like this. But the stream shrinks to a trickle or less during every dry spell. We'd get power for a few weeks a year, then we'd look at ugly plastic pipe the rest of the time. Diverting the flow would surely affect the character of the stream and the vegetation surrounding it. Would we lose the caddisfly larvae the birds come to pick up down by the marsh? Would the moss and skunk cabbage dry up on the upper banks? We could have a huge influence on this small area. What happened to living gently in the wilderness?

Tom says half the idea of living out here is to get off fossil fuels, and hydropower would help us do that. There might not be enough water pressure to make a system work, but he'd like to try. I can't believe he'd disturb the stream for such small potential gain. I want to live in beautiful surroundings. I want our setting to be as natural as possible. How can our visions of life out here be so different?

September 2 – I'm solo at the cabin, halfway through a week I set aside to focus on writing. At last it's stopped raining, and I'm sitting on the deck of the main cabin looking out at the mouth of the bay. Lynn Canal—is it truly the world's longest fjord?—stretches north toward Haines. Two fishing boats carve streams of white foam on a river of molten pewter. A line of puffy clouds is moving south on a layer of clear air. The sky is filled with piles of pillow stuffing heaped on a conveyor belt headed toward the open Pacific. I wonder how many other masses of air, with different temperatures and different moisture content, are lying or moving above my holdfast at the water's edge. There must be patchworks and tangled skeins of them up there, and we're seldom even aware of them.

You don't see the world on this scale in very many places. From our windows in town I see maybe a few hundred feet—to trees, clumps of huckleberry and highbush cranberry, and the house next door. Here I look at salt water, mountains, islands, forests on the far shore, marble reefs in front of the cabin, a beach that changes with every shift of tide, a grassy meadow and a pond with dragonflies, spruce and alder forest around the cabin, and the magical little stream that burbles in different voices depending on the weather.

It's the richness and diversity of this place that seems so precious—the chance to see so many different kinds of landscape and the plants and wildlife that flourish in each one. I'll spend the rest of my life trying to learn more about them.

November 20 – "What do you do out there?" The pilot who dropped me off on our beach last week asked me that. Then yesterday, when Kathee called from town to ask why I'd missed the monthly retirees' lunch confab, she said—delicately, of course—"and what projects do you have going on out there?" She laughed when I told her about doing laundry in two 5-gallon buckets.

Then she wanted to know if there were other people around—and what will we do if we run out of food? I told her about the folks living full-time at the head of the bay, and the hunters in the cabin above the sandy beach this week, and that we could have groceries sent out on the weekly mail plane if we needed them. I said I was working on the cabin book, splitting wood for the hot-water heater, studying lichens, writing in my journal, making bread, and writing poetry for my writer's group in town. She seemed to think that sounded like a full enough schedule.

November 28 – A fierce northerly this morning, but Tom was determined to take the skiff up-bay to meet Phil and look for deer. I bundled up in my fleece jacket and chest waders, and went down to help him launch off the beach against the wind. The skiff lurched and crashed as 3-foot-high waves broke at our knees, and the water splashed against my chest and face. We shoved the skiff out into the waves, but Tom couldn't pole fast enough against the wind, and the boat nearly blew against the rocks. I heard the engine sputter to life, but when the bow turned into the wind, a gust lifted it, and I thought the boat was going to flip over. Tom just lurched to one side to level it and kept going.

It's hard to fault Tom's judgment, which hasn't let us down yet, but I hate feeling helpless when a situation feels precarious. Well, it was his decision. I'd brought my binoculars so I could watch his progress up the bay, but what good was that? I'd be too far away to help if the boat flipped or the engine failed. Even if I ran back to the cabin and called Phil, would he hear the CB or the phone? And how long would it take him to launch his skiff to make a rescue? I doubted Tom could swim to shore in his hip boots. At least he had put on the self-inflating life vest I bought him in October. I watched as he motored at last into the lee of the big island. Guess he made it this time. I turned back toward the cabin. I'll have bacon and onions ready in case there's venison liver for dinner.

December 15 – It's ten years now since we started building this cabin. Looking back, I can see how many of our ideas and attitudes have changed. At first we tried to cut as few trees as possible. It almost hurt to watch big, stately alders crash down to make room for the cabin. It pained me to hack out ferns and moss and whole networks of roots that might have taken decades to develop. But much of what we wanted to see—the bay and what was happening on it, sunsets, weather changes, wildlife —was out on the beach or somewhere beyond. We wanted to watch herons, loons, murrelets, eagles, otters, mink, and sea ducks. We wanted to hear the whales. In years when bears were plentiful, we needed to see if the beach was clear before we walked to the skiff or the beach gardens.

So every year we cut a few more small trees and branches. We still have clusters of spruce, hemlock, and alders sheltering us from the water. We have good views of wildlife and boat traffic. And we can see bears approaching from either direction along the beach. We can even sit on the front deck and watch humpbacks spout and breach at the mouth of the bay.

In our first starry-eyed dreams, we thought the original cabin, 17 by 25 feet, would be plenty of space for the two of us. The life we imagined would be pretty simple, and hadn't thousands of pioneers done it before us? But we needed tools, and supplies, and outdoor gear. We decided to install more comforts. Suddenly the 12-foot-square living-dining room had to accommodate a wood-fired hot-water heater and a 20-gallon hot-water storage tank. The 10-foot-square bedroom needed a closet, not just a few pegs on the wall. The dining room table couldn't accommodate my writing projects and three meals a day. And when our families came to visit, even just in twos and threes, they weren't particularly cozy camped on the futon and a folding cot scrunched between the wood stove and the folded-up dinner table.

So "the cabin" has turned into a small complex. We now have the 16- by 20-foot addition for my workspace and guest quarters, a 14- by 16-foot workshop for Tom, an 8- by 12-foot shed for the diesel generator, a pole barn to house the tractor, and two woodsheds too full to make room for splits from the teetering alder we need to cut down. For a "complex," it's still simple, but it's lots more than we envisioned at first.

When we built the original cabin we wanted to do everything ourselves, for the thrill of doing it, and because we were figuring out what to do as we went along. By the time we started work on the addition, we were ready to accept when friends and family offered to help with roofing, or cutting insulation, or staining exterior walls during a tiny window of sunny weather. Eventually, too, we'd both had our fill of hauling heavy loads up the beach. When Tom found the little Kubota tractor for sale in town, it seemed like a good solution. I dislike its rumbling engine, the diesel fumes, and the sight of tracks on the beach. But I no longer begrudge its place here, especially when I think of us living here in our seventies and eighties. There doesn't seem much sense anymore in carrying 10 sheets of plywood or 45 lengths of metal roofing up the beach when we can stack them in the bucket of the tractor and save our energy for fishing or planting potatoes.

A big change for me has been in the idea of wilderness. We dreamed of building a wilderness cabin, but here we are with neighbors in a landscape that people have been using for hundreds of years. Besides, once you build a cabin you're not in wilderness anymore, are you?

We've left the woods surrounding us as natural as possible, but Tom wants to extend the tractor road to the back of the lot so we can gather more wood. He hasn't given up the idea of a hydroplant. And I keep wanting to remake things to fit my own ideas of beauty, however "natural." When we dug up big clumps of ferns as we cleared for buildings, I often replanted them at the bases of trees or in places where there was bare ground. I thought the downed logs and freshlycut stumps in the front yard looked harsh and barren, so I gathered clumps of moss from logs in the woods and transplanted them over the bare spots. One day I found a big clump of star flowers—those tiny stems with whorls of leaves and delicate white blossoms—along the path up from the beach. They were so beautiful I arranged a circle of rocks next to an old stump and made a garden I can see from my office window.

Every year we've planted rhubarb and lettuce and potatoes, and I've transplanted daffodils and foxglove Donna culled from her gardens. I hauled those flat rocks from across the bay to make steppingstone paths that keep us above the muck during fall rains.

I'm not sure how much we'll change things in the years ahead. More folks than Tom's dad have said, since we put in a kitchen with cabinets and running water, "This isn't a cabin anymore. It's a house." But it's still a cabin to me. It's compact and simple. It's rustic. It's off the grid, and we built it ourselves. Most of all, it's a place where life slows down and you have time to look at the natural world around you.

I'd like to think that, even with all these changes, somehow we're fitting in with the overall landscape. For sure we're not just barreling in and completely remaking things, but we're not just standing aside afraid to touch anything either. We're making the place our own— nesting, but still trying to fit in. That's the whole idea, isn't it?

8.

Four Walls
against the Wind

2006

July 10 – At last we have columbines—three colors of blooms from seedlings Donna gave me from her garden last summer. Despite limited sunlight beneath all the trees, the plants have flourished in the round garden beyond my writing desk window. Every color reminds me how much I love these flowers: dark purple blossoms, like those we found near Echo Cove to make a birthday bouquet for Tom's mom; bright pink blooms like the ones along Perseverance Trail; and on the dwarf plant, which Donna had said might not even grow, the palest pink flowers, like the ones in the bed next to Donna's blackberries. The plant Helen Peck gave me from her yard has ten reddish, salmon-pink blossoms with yellow centers, like the ones that grow on the ledges out past the rocky point; and the little plant I put in the hollow center of a rotting stump has leaves, though no blossoms as yet.

Yesterday I saw a hummingbird feeding at the purple blossoms. If I can get more of these flowers to grow, we might have more little bird visitors, too.

As Tom and I ate breakfast today two yearling deer walked right through the yard. They are so finely made— long necks and bodies on such slender legs. They stretch their necks out, their noses trembling. Their eyes roll back as if they're ready to bolt. One leads the way, the other follows but stops to nibble a fern. Their tails flick as they meander along.

They came along the beach path from the north and followed my flagstone steps along the stream. How close to the cabin would they come? I rushed to the back bedroom, and there they were, mincing past Tom's workshop just a few feet from the window, and sniffing nervously. They look different in their reddish-brown summer coats, not gray like when we hunt them in the fall; but they still have the lovely white patches on their noses, and black and white on their tails. Yesterday I saw where deer had nipped big chunks out of devil's club leaves on the beach ledge. They'd nipped the dead flower heads from my iris, too. Was this pair on its second trip through?

July 12 – This morning about 11 a.m. I found two slime molds on the main trail behind the cabin. Both look like small clumps of cauliflower—tapioca slime maybe? Decided to look in the area where I found scrambled egg slime last year, and Bingo! I found a clump of what could have been somebody's breakfast omelet at the top of the hill behind the workshop. The clump was as wide as my two hands outstretched, thumb to thumb, and you could see white threads of slime around the perimeter. The cauliflower slimes were on a live hemlock and a small rotting stump. This one was on a mossy mound of ground with an old stump rotting underneath it.

July 14 – More slime molds. Found more of the gray tapioca type on the north end of the lot. The smooth, grayish-looking lumps look the way the cauliflower-shaped ones I found two days ago look today. Found another big patch of scrambled eggs on the hill just a few feet north of the other patch. This clump is bright yellow, very fresh looking, and the size of a very large dinner plate. The original scrambled egg has turned dirty yellow-orange and is losing its shape as if it were melting.

July 16 – More slimes! Last night, when Larry and his nephew Lew escorted me home from dinner at Larry and Angela's place, I took them along the back path and onto the knoll to see my "discoveries." They seemed really interested when I told them how slimes begin as little spores that creep around and feed on bacteria and decaying organic matter, and how the spores can be shaped like little crawling amoebas, but if they land in water, or get covered with water, they develop whiplike appendages to help them move around. I'd love to see slimes growing so fast they seem to be creeping across the ground, as some people reported in two different magazine articles I read; but these apparently stationary ones are fascinating enough. It's amazing to think the spores hang around in the woods till some environmental or chemical signal prompts them to come together into what are supposedly single-celled masses with millions or billions of nuclei. When Bob Armstrong and I researched them for an *Alaskan Southeaster* article, we even found serious speculation about possible medical breakthroughs because the way slimes change form like that is something like the way human embryo cells differentiate into cells to form various types of structures and organs. What a wonder sitting right in our back yard.

July 18 – Cloudy, 53 degrees. It rained all night, and everything is soaked. Where are the "three good dry days" we need before I can start re-staining the north wall of the cabin? I'd hoped to have it done before Tom comes out from town next Friday. Decided instead to explore the sandy beach and the rock ledges along the southeast side of the bay. I packed for a real expedition. Took rain gear, knife, cell phone, extra fleece shirt, notebook and pens, 10X hand lens, small bottle of water, a granola bar, and some dried mangoes, all crammed into my day pack. Camera went into my pocket, binocs around my neck. I carried the shotgun, which seemed a little silly since hardly anyone's spotted bears this year. Still, it's better to be safe. Hiked the trail through the woods past the other cabins, crossed both streams at Bear Heaven, and scrunched across the sandbar to the beach. Saw three deer feeding in the beach meadow, two mergansers and a few gulls at the mouth of Bear Creek, and a small Dungeness crab hunkered down in a sandy-bottomed tide pool. The low-tide beach was deserted except for scattered fronds of leathery brown kelp and an assortment of washed-up shells.

It took twenty minutes to cross the beach, then it was tough going over the rocks till I reached the outcrop below the cliffs, where I'd hoped to find wildflowers. Found some sort of daisies with fifteen to eighteen white petals and knobby yellow centers, wild geranium with glowing purple blossoms, and what I think is villous cinquefoil already gone to yellow-green seed pods. Some of the yarrow flowers here are pink as well as white, and I found a wild iris with one elegant dark purple bloom. A few straggly spruce trees hang down over the cliff's edge, and plants struggle for footholds in crevices and crannies. I climbed up the rock face following a small ravine and found otter trails and scat, and a large deposit of bear droppings at the top. The forest is very open there with hardly any understory beneath pole-size spruce and hemlock. A game trail broad enough for bear winds along the cliff about 10 feet back from the edge. I'll enjoy walking on the rocky beach below more now that I know what it's like up on top.

Back down on the rocks I scrambled along shore just above the rockweed and barnacle level, and finally reached the gravelly pocket beach inside the entrance to the bay. Here the land dropped lower, and the trees overhanging the beach were alders. Tall grass grew thick beneath the trees, and cow parsnip reared white flower heads on stalks as high as my shoulder. I found drift logs covered with moss, patches of Cladonia lichen with stalks like tiny trumpets in amongst it, and spruce seedlings only an inch tall getting a start in the protective moss. This cove must be sheltered from north and south winds and warmer than the cliffsides. More soil has collected here, too. What a difference in environment within a few hundred feet.

Ate my dried mango and granola bar lunch and headed back toward the cabin, content with my explorations. This time, though, as I walked across the sandy beach, I noticed thousands of little hollow brown spouts sticking up above the sand, just like the ones we have on our beach. Then I realized I could hear them—or something down there with them in the sand. All around me I heard a snap, crackle, and pop like Rice Crispies in a bowl of milk. But there were two distinct sounds—the staccato crackle-tat-tat and a faint, repeated squeaking like the sound of a tiny screen door opening and closing. If only I were small enough to squeeze down between those grains of sand, then I could see what kind of critters were welcoming the incoming tide like that. There's a whole world down there that I haven't even begun to learn about. How am I going to fit all this exploration into a lifetime?

Back at the cabin I indulged in some hot mint tea and shortbread, but apparently Ma Nature was not through with me yet. On my way to the beach to pump rain water out of the skiff, I was stopped short in the beach fringe by a fluttering mob of songbirds. Small, gray, skittering birds I felt sure were kinglets flicked

among the branches of the spruce tree just ahead of
me. Then one flew across my path at chin level, landed
in a small alder just past my elbow, and flashed a bright
red crest. A ruby-crowned kinglet for sure. It hopped
among the branches and grabbed something in its bill,
then flew back to the spruce tree. It approached one of
the other birds, which was making faint, high-pitched
kinglet squeaks, and stuffed the insect into its mouth.
So . . . it was an adult feeding its young—and a male at
that.

Some other small birds fluttered and ran along
the ground. I saw flashes of white outer tail feathers:
juncos. Some were brown-streaked without the adult
brown back and dark hood. More youngsters. Beyond
all this activity I saw more movement. Five robins went
parading across the beach meadow. Something smaller
than a robin flashed past my feet onto a chunk of driftwood, and I saw the brown-spotted chest and light eye
ring of a hermit thrush. Then my eye caught movement
back in the trees. Four small brownish birds with creamy
breasts were spiraling up the trunks of several alders.
They must have been brown creepers, and if there were
four together, some were probably young ones. I heard
wings rush overhead as two woodpeckers fluttered and
landed 20 feet up in the canopy. What was going on?
This was a full-fledged invasion! The woodpeckers were
deep red over their heads and breasts—our friends the
sapsuckers. I watched them skitter and peck at several
alder trunks, then they mewed twice and flew away.

How could there be more than this? But there was.
Beyond the robins, far down the meadow, a song sparrow
churred—a watery burble. And back in the woods the
hooligan ravens cawed in loud screeches way out of

proportion to the delicate birds close around me.

Next thing I knew, the whole flock of songbirds had moved on, fluttering through the beach fringe toward the head of the bay. Only the robins and the ravens stayed behind. Ten minutes more of tea and cookies and I'd have missed this whole, wonderful scene, but I guess today I was fated to be lucky.

I need to make one more entry today, if only as a reminder that some days out here wildlife sightings come almost faster than we can absorb them. After splitting some kindling and emptying the compost, I turned on my laptop and went to work at my writing desk. But when I looked out the front window, I spotted a merganser and her single large chick out on the reef. They were hunkered down on the rocks, moving just a few inches higher every few minutes as the tide came in. Hadn't these birds figured out the tides yet? Or did they begrudge moving? Or did they not mind having to move every few minutes? Time and again the waves came close enough to lap at their flanks. Then, just before the water reached them, they'd stand up. They'd fluff their wings, creep a few inches higher on the rocks, wiggle as if settling into the softest of feather beds, then gaze out at the water again. A few more waves, another move, just a few inches again. How many times would they move? How long would they hold out before swimming away? Five harlequin ducks were paddling and diving nearby, and I was surprised when the merganser chick—apparently more aggressive than its mother—leaped off the reef and lunged at the ducks. The harlequins scuttled away, just out of reach, and the chick clambered to its rocky perch again. The mergansers held out for an hour, giving ground in the most parsimonious of increments. Then

I got absorbed in writing, and the world at arm's length took over. When I looked up, both the mergansers and the harlequins were gone.

July 25 – Tom came out from town Friday on the mail plane. He'd hardly put his feet on the ground before he started working on his hydroplant. He's made a catchment barrel and put it in the pool where the water collects before flowing down out of the muskeg. The barrel's pretty well hidden by tall grass and brush, but I can't summon up my usual encouragement and enthusiasm for this project. I'd hoped he'd be discouraged by having to plow through the brush and uneven ground to lay pipe along the stream, but he seems determined to do it. Yesterday he began hauling armloads of pipe back there and connecting the pieces into a solid line. The pipe comes in 10-foot lengths, but some of it is broken pieces he salvaged from somewhere in town. I figure it will take sixty or seventy pieces to get all the way down to the foot of the stream. I'm not offering to help.

July 26 – John and Lucy are visiting, and as always are helping with projects around the cabin. Today the three of us helped Tom carry the rest of the pipe up the stream toward the catchment barrel. It wasn't much fun stumbling through the woods and over the lumpy, soft ground. Every length of pipe I carried seemed determined to bang against a tree or snag in a patch of brush. Lucy saw I was grumpy, but she tried to help me laugh it off. She said Tom, Suzi, and Rob were always coming up with big projects like this when they were kids. As the older sister, Lucy was of course above all that. But that's what kids do, isn't it—try to pull off things that everyone else thinks are impossible. Tom's not a kid anymore, but he still loves that kind of challenge.

With four of us hauling, we finally got all the pipe lengths spread out along the stream, and Tom walked along snapping the pieces together without clomping through the stream as much as I'd feared. Within a couple of hours we had pipe laid all the way to the marsh near the mouth of the stream. The pipe was as ugly as I'd expected, and I hated seeing it plunked down there among the little forest plants and hummocks of moss. Still, it was hard not to feel a sense of jubilation when Tom opened the control valve and water started flowing down into the catchment cups of the old Pelton wheel he'd set up.

The flow of water was pretty meager, and Tom was disappointed that he didn't get more volume and pressure. All afternoon he fiddled with the Pelton wheel set-up, trying different sizes of nozzles and making adjustments none of the rest of us understood.

July 27 – Tom announced at breakfast this morning that it doesn't appear the hydroplant will work. Our little stream just doesn't have enough volume or elevation drop to build adequate pressure to turn the wheel. He's being very philosophical about it. He'd said all along that there probably wasn't much chance it would work, but he wanted to try. John and Lucy and I helped him disassemble the pipes, haul them out of the woods, and stack them behind the generator shed. I felt sorry for Tom's sake, but I was so glad the experiment didn't work. For me it would have changed our beautiful woodland setting to something like what you see behind the railroad yards in cities Back East.

Maybe Tom will have an opportunity to try his idea someplace else. If anyone else in the bay ever wants to try a hydroplant, he'll have plenty of know-how and materials to contribute. There are bigger streams than ours that have no fish in them, and they drop from higher ground, so maybe Tom will get to put everything he's learned to good use some other time.

September 4 – We're waiting out bad weather in town and loading up for the coming week at the cabin. This week's project will be installing six new batteries—marine deep-cycle ones—to replace a couple that have gone bad in our power storage system. It will be no mean feat to get the darn things out there. They look like huge lunch pails and weigh 120 pounds each. A woman at the marine supply store loaded all six onto a pallet and used a forklift to put them into the bed of our pickup. At the harbor, our friend Mitch had his forklift handy, and he offered to move the whole pallet out of our pickup to the top of the boat ramp. Tom unstrapped the batteries from the pallet and put them onto two carts, then we dragged them down the ramp and along the dock to the boat. As luck would have it, we ran into Sam and Andy loading lumber for a trip to their cabins, and they insisted on helping Tom lift the batteries over the gunwales and into the cockpit. What a relief. I could not have helped, and I was really worried Tom would hurt his back manhandling those things from an awkward position.

September 6 – The wind's down to 15 knots today, so we headed *Dauntless* out to the cabin. We'd no sooner pulled into the bay and tied up at the float than here came our friends Sam and Marshall in their skiff. They'd been watching for us since yesterday, and they insisted on helping unload the batteries back out of the cockpit, onto the float, and into our skiff. They followed as we motored the quarter mile to our beach, waited while

Tom drove the tractor down to tide level, then helped him load the batteries into the tractor bucket. The little Kubota hauled the batteries up the beach, but the path is too narrow for it to go all the way to the workshop, so the three guys had to carry each battery the last 70 feet.

This is one of several times I've been bowled over by the way people just step forward to help out here, even when you wouldn't have asked them to. Nobody seems to keep score, but it's nice to think you'll be able to lend a hand sometime later on. Heaven knows we all have enough projects out here that require lots of muscle, more than a little ingenuity, or both.

September 8 – Sam said we could help ourselves to the trees cut down when the tractor road was extended through the woods behind the cabin. That inspired Tom to build a new woodshed that we'll try to fill this fall. No need to haul lumber from town this time. Tom cut and peeled about thirty flagpole-size hemlocks from around the cabin, and made a 12-foot-square open framework with notched diagonal bracing. The roof is of metal roofing we salvaged when we had the house in town reroofed year before last. It's gratifying to use it after all the work of hauling it out here. I think Tom's enjoyed the challenge of using nearly all natural materials; besides, he says we built the entire shed for the cost of the screws and nails that hold it together.

Today we worked together to start our first stack. We found a big downed hemlock, still solid and with tiny, close-set growth rings. The trunk was only about 14 inches across, but it must have had at least a hundred annual rings. They were so fine and closely packed I couldn't count them. There were no other big trees or stumps nearby, so we imagined that perhaps it was very poor soil rather than being shaded that caused the tree to grow so slowly. I wondered if it had once been at the fringe of the muskeg that's now about 200 yards away.

Tom cut the trunk into stove lengths and split them, and I carried them in the wheelbarrow and stacked them in the new shed. I thought as I was working that there was nowhere else I would rather be and nothing else I would rather be doing. What was it I was so happy about?

It was comfortably cool and not raining, for one thing, and there were no bugs. The air smelled clean and earthy, and it felt good to be exercising (and maybe working off the chocolate cake we'd had for lunch). Tom and I worked in perfect rhythm, and I was glad we had the skills and stamina to fend for ourselves in yet one more basic way out here. After a number of trips pushing the wheelbarrow along the path I'd made, I started noticing the forest around me. I'd often written that area off as almost a dead zone. It has small and medium-size spruce and hemlock growing so close together they pretty much close out sky and sun. The light under the trees seems dark and gloomy, and the ground is mostly brown duff broken by small sprouts of menzesia, blueberry and huckleberry, and here and there the pretty deep green of rattlesnake plantain. But as I stopped to scrape together dirt and rotting wood to beef up my path, I found three different kinds of moss. It grew in patches over every broken-off stump, fallen log, or exposed tree root—pale green like clusters of feathery fingers, deep dark green in a kind of knobby velvet coat, and shiny green made of tiny round leaves with hairlike stalks. Some of the most decayed stumps had turned brick red and were crumbling into soil. Around one of them a patch of single delight (*Pyrola uniflora*, a wintergreen) lifted slender stalks from ground-hugging clusters of shiny round leaves. I could see round white seed pods at the tops of stems that a month ago must have formed a miniature forest of nodding greenish-white blossoms—blossoms that would have tipped downward, in the way that makes the plant's other nickname—"shy maiden"—seem so well-chosen.

Not only that: some of the rattlesnake plantain were in bloom. From each rosette of dark green leaves a pale, slender stalk stuck straight up, displaying a neat row of tiny bell-shaped flowers—miniature orchids, all facing the same direction. This wasn't a dead zone after all. I just needed the time and inclination to look—a lesson I've learned how many times now?

September 9 –Three bears on our beach as we were finishing dinner about 7:30 p.m.—a smallish black sow with two 1-1/2-year-old cubs, which are also both black. They came meandering along the high-high tide line, appearing suddenly from beyond the big rock by the garden barrels.

Their shoulder muscles and humps seem to roll as they walk. The cubs ramble along with the sow as their center. What I think we find so awesome about the way bears walk is partly an effect of their bulk. They're stodgy, thick, heavy-bodied, and heavy-legged. They're built close to the ground, like a car or a freight train. You sense momentum, and so much power and weight it's difficult to stop. They're like a tractor trailer: weight and bulk moving in a direct line. Even when you startle a bear, it seems reluctant to change direction. Yes, they can move like lightning, but that hasn't been their first response most of the times I've seen them.

These three bears did not seem menacing or malicious. In fact, they seemed oblivious to anything outside themselves. I suppose in a sense they can be oblivious, since they're at the top of the local food chain, with no predators but human beings to be afraid of. The sow flipped up a chunk of ground and nosed into the silverweed patch—*zap!* One flick of the paw and a chunk of dirt the size of a baseball spun two feet away. She stuck her nose down, getting the silverweed root, I guess.

Both the cubs sniffed and bit at the outhaul line, but it didn't sustain their interest. One cub lumbered into my garden at the base of the wind generator pole. It mowed down iris and bachelor's buttons, and pulled over the driftwood I'd stacked up to form a kind of backdrop. The other pawed at the base of a skunk cabbage plant, breaking off two big leaves and exposing the white underground stem.

Bears seem like other powerful forces of nature—floods, tides, storms, wind. They just barrel along doing their thing, and if you happen to be in their way—plant, log, rock, whatever—they just roll over you, leaving little pockets of havoc in their wake.

At one point the sow looked up toward the cabin as if she was curious. She sniffed the air and raised up partway on her back legs. I hoped she wasn't going to come closer so we'd have to respond, but Tom had had enough. He thinks the bears need to learn to stay away from the cabin. He went out onto the deck with a thumper round in the shotgun and yelled, "Hup, Bear! Go on. Get outa here." The sow looked startled and turned away, walking slow and stiff-legged for a few steps. When Tom yelled again, she half-ran through the beach fringe, and both cubs took off after her. I was relieved the cubs ran and the sow decided not to mount a challenge.

September 9 – A 19.7 high tide at 2:00 this afternoon. The water is up 6 feet past the outhaul poles and has nearly reached the potato barrel closest to the water. The little pond and all but the top 10 feet of the beach meadow are flooded. The seed heads of the tall, tawny-colored grass wave gracefully above the swells of water enveloping them. The bright green dune grass, with its wider blades, is lying down and floating on the water. It will be beaten down in round, swirling patches when the water recedes.

I love seeing the water high like this. It's almost like living on a lakeshore—a closeness to the water we don't usually get. With heavy clouds and a low ceiling, it's dark even now at the height of the day. I'm more than content to be indoors writing and tending a cozy fire in the new wood stove. What luxury to have a glass door so we can see the flames and watch their color and hypnotic flickering.

Tom's disgusted with the weather. He's finally given in and stretched a big tarp over the two spruce logs he's trying to cut into lumber. It turns out their diameter is too big for the width of the guide blade on his chainsaw sawmill, so he had to cut a sliver off one side, then lift the log with the tractor and turn it a quarter round to take a sliver off the second side. He'll have to do that two more times, I guess, before he can begin cutting boards.

September 20 – Rain, rain, rain. It's tiresome, but we're trying to work anyway. Yesterday we cut and hauled more hemlock to the new shed before we gave up, drenched to the bone. This morning I hauled five wheelbarrow loads of seaweed off the beach before the worst of the showers moved in. In the beach mud I found a bear track the size of a large dinner plate. It must have been made since the last high tide. In the beach meadow I also found bear trails on both sides of the big rock where the ravens perch. Both trails led to and from large patches of flattened grass where a bear may have stopped for a nap.

Tom encountered a black sow and a yearling cub (a very roly-poly one, he said) as he walked back to the road to pick up some last splits of wood before lunch. When he yelled, the sow ran back down the road, then into the brush; but the cub just stood still looking startled, as if wondering where its mother had gone. When the cub stood up and looked at him, Tom worried that it might be curious and come toward him as one did a couple of years ago. But apparently it heard its mother thrashing around in the brush, and it turned and ran toward her instead. We'd carried the shotgun with us all morning while we were working, but when we decided to quit for lunch we propped it up in the woodshed, and all Tom had with him was a hatchet. So much for being prepared for bear encounters.

September 24 – Yesterday morning Tom nearly got creamed. Just as he came out the door of his workshop, a large hawk went careening past, streaking full speed through the cleared path between the cabin and the generator shed. Tom ducked, and all he glimpsed was a big brown bird whizzing through the open space like a plane in a wind tunnel. Today we saw a female harrier swooping across the meadow. I suppose the hawks are following the migrating songbirds.

November 19 – Missed getting out to the cabin this week. It's been snowing and blowing in Juneau for two weeks. Phil said a neighbor who had come out to his cabin to go hunting has been trying to get a flight back to town, but no small planes will brave the wind and poor visibility, and apparently it's even too blustery for a helicopter. It's good to remember there are times like this every winter.

November 29 – Finally flew out to the cabin yesterday and got a good lesson in the kinds of obstacles the weather can throw at you during the winter months here. The flight shouldn't have been difficult. The winds were southerly in town, and were not overly strong. But once we got over the bay, the wind was gusting out of the north. That meant, since it was also low tide, we couldn't land on our beach; the wind would have blown the plane sideways and pushed it into the rocks. Tom suggested that the pilot should land us in the cove about a quarter mile north of the cabin, where there was at least minimal shelter from the wind. Unfortunately, gusts blew us north of the deep water area, the floats scraped to a stop 50 yards from shore, and the plane was grounded till we could remove our weight and the weight of our gear. I had on my chest waders, and Tom was wearing hip boots, so we just climbed out and started unloading our stuff. It took each of us two trips, sloshing through knee-deep water and slipping on slimy rocks, but we finally got everything to the beach: four plastic tubs of groceries, both our packs, my laptop computer in its case, one insulated cooler bag, a 5-gallon jug of drinking water, and some boards Tom had brought to finish some project or other. Almost immediately the plane got off the water and took off into the wind.

The beach above high-tide line was heaped with snow whipped into bizarre patterns of drifts and nearly bare ground. We stashed our gear behind a big rock, then grabbed my computer and any fresh groceries that might tempt an errant bear and headed for the cabin. The trail was clear enough, but the snow was knee deep most of the way, Three drifts were so high we had to circle through the woods to get around them. I was bushed by the time we reached the cabin, but we got inside just fine and started a fire to start the long settling-in process.

The first order of the day was to get the skiff floating so we could go pick up the rest of our food and gear before high tide. That meant dragging the skiff on its trailer a good 300 feet from the tractor shed to the beach. The first 30 feet went fine, then skiff and trailer bogged down into a gigantic snowdrift that had built up across the trail. Tom got out our one snow shovel, and I grabbed a dustpan, and we started scooping away the snow. It was like trying to empty a bathtub with a teaspoon. Tom said, "This is crazy. I'm going to go start the tractor. We'll use the bucket to clear a path to the beach." I stayed and kept shoveling in case the tractor didn't start.

Well, the tractor didn't start. It turned over once or twice, then died. We went back to man- and woman-power and got about half the drift shoveled down. That gave us enough leeway to slide the skiff off the trailer, over the drift, and across the snow at the top of the beach to the gravel cleared by the last high tide. Tom went back and carried the trailer over, we slid the skiff back onto it, then we pushed the skiff and trailer another 50 feet down to the water and launched it.

Unfortunately, during the snow removal project the wind had increased, and there were 3-foot waves crashing on the beach. We couldn't clip the skiff on and pull it out on the outhaul because the outhaul line was frozen down for about 10 feet where the stream had overflowed—another contingency we hadn't expected. I held the skiff while Tom dragged the trailer back up above tide level; then we both climbed into the boat and used the frozen outhaul line to pull ourselves into water that was deep enough so that we could start the outboard.

We beat our way over to the little cove, crashing bow-first into waves and wallowing in the troughs, but I was grateful the spray that splashed over us was not freezing. When we got to the beach, I held the skiff off the rocks while Tom ran up to the big rock and retrieved our gear. He had to make three trips in all. We used what we'd learned to get off that beach, too: our neighbor's outhaul, which was close by, was frozen down just as ours had been, so we used that line to pull ourselves out into deep water, then started the engine for the bronco ride home.

Back on our beach I again held the skiff off the rocks while Tom ran up to get an ax to hack through the ice and free the outhaul. It seemed to take forever. The waves didn't look any bigger now, but they were splashing against me nearly waist high, and the wind felt like ice. My fleece coat was soaked, but my good old Cabela's Neoprene waders kept me dry. Tom finally got the outhaul line free, and we yanked it through the pulleys, beating at chunks of ice and scraping off globs of frozen seaweed as it pulled the skiff away from the rocks to the safety of deep water.

Up in the cabin we changed into dry clothes. Tom had gotten soaked where water splashed above his hip boots, and my fleece coat was frozen shut so I had to climb out of it with the zipper halfway down. I set about unpacking our stuff, while Tom went to deal with the problem of water. We'd disconnected the water line on our last trip, and the water we'd stored in 5-gallon plastic buckets was frozen solid. Tom got two chunks of ice out of the plastic buckets, and we started melting them in stainless steel pots on top of the wood stove. After a trip into the crawl space, he found the copper pipes were not frozen; it was the 55-gallon plastic storage barrels that were solid ice. So we had a chance of getting running water at least into the kitchen, but it would probably take a few days.

Outdoors you could sure see where the wind and snow had raised havoc. There were drifts all over the yard, even where the buildings should have broken the thrust of the wind. The outhouse door had blown open, and the little building was filled with packed and drifted snow. Snow had even swirled around the back deck of the main cabin and packed hard a good 2 inches thick on our stack of stove wood. We cleaned things up as well as we could and decided to leave the rest.

After an easy supper—beans and hot dogs—we spent the evening reading and monitoring the ice-melting project. The floor and walls of our little ice palace were still cold, but by bedtime the flannel sheets had warmed up, and I'm sure things will look better by morning.

November 30 – More snow coming down this morning, blowing across the front yard like smoke, and rolling in like clumps of white tumbleweed from a few feet off the beach. I went onto the front deck to stand in it, and it's fine and dry even though the temperature has warmed up to 27 degrees. Tom got the tractor running and cleared a road to the beach. He looked like a machine out of Star Wars, lumbering around in an arctic waste with swirls of white whipping around him. I find myself wanting to shovel everywhere, clearing both decks and making trails through the drifts to the compost piles, the woodsheds, even Pops' rocky ledge with its overlook of the bay. I suppose it's an impulse to break out of confinement and feel as though you have at least a little control over your surroundings.

The wind knocked over a big spruce tree in the beach fringe just south of the new woodshed. The tree's roots are tipped up perpendicular to the ground, and they look to have grown not more than 4 or 5 inches into the soil. Apparently this tree was not hooked into that network where roots overlap and help to hold each other up against the wind. I wonder if that would have saved it.

Midnight: the snow has stopped, and there are pinpricks of stars. Above the bay we can see northern lights—streaks and patches of pale green fleeting across the sky.

December first tomorrow. Winter feels long, and it's hardly begun. Tom's counting twenty-three more days till winter solstice, when the sun will turn around. I think we'll both dance on the beach to celebrate that this year.

December 1 – Tom built a Styrofoam box around the water barrels, packed it with towels, and put a kerosene lantern inside. Voila! We have running water in the kitchen. The ice in the storage barrels will probably melt slowly, though, so we are still collecting snow and ice for the aluminum pots on the stove. Melting the snow, then straining spruce needles and scraps of leaves and grass out of the water, is time-consuming, but we have plenty now to heat for dishes and washing up.

8:15 p.m. - Suddenly the wind's come up. It was perfectly still fifteen minutes ago when I walked out to the studio. Now the wind is roaring across the waves, ringing the chimes on the end of the cabin, and making the wind generator howl. I went out onto the front deck to feel and hear the gusts. Being here is different from being in town. Not only are we exposed to weather coming across large stretches of water, but the cabin's small, so we're more aware when something changes, and it's easy to step outside and walk right into it. Away from town and all its facilities, there's the slightest edge of danger, too. If something happens we're on our own. But that's okay. We've made that choice.

December 2 – Whew! Yesterday's Weather Bureau forecast was right. We're getting a full-blown winter storm. Snow is blasting across the beach and through the yard, and the wind generator sounds like a dump truck laboring up a steep hill. Snow is splattered all over the windows and heaped up in down-curving arcs at the bottoms. I feel as if I'm sitting in a Currier and Ives painting. Curled up with my hot buttered rum and a good book, I feel as contented as Tom looks sitting in his recliner with the latest issue of *Guns and Ammo*.

I've been reviewing old journals, and yesterday I found an entry from July 1995. The cabin wasn't closed in then, and we were hunkered down in *Dauntless* waiting out a storm. I remember feeling relatively safe tied up at the state float while the wind bounced us around and whistled against the windows. But I feel a lot safer here. Our foothold in the wilderness is anchored pretty deep now. I think our roots are entwined with the natural and human ones that hold this place steady. We've got our foundation—no, we've got more. We've got four walls and a roof—several roofs. We've got a stout home base from which we can venture out and explore, and the world has more than enough wonders to intrigue us for a lifetime. With a little luck maybe we'll withstand all the rest of the gales the weather throws at us—here in this place we've both come so far to make our home.

LaVergne, TN USA
27 December 2009
168062LV00002B/72/P